WRITING AND SELLING
A NONFICTION BOOK

Writing
and Selling
a Nonfiction Book

by Max Gunther

Boston · THE WRITER, Inc. · Publishers

Library of Congress Catalog Card Number 75-188591

ISBN: 0-87116-074-9

U.S. Library of Congress Cataloging in Publication Data

Gunther, Max, 1927 —
Writing and selling a nonfiction book.

1. Authorship. I. Title.
PN145.G8   1973   808'.02   75-188591
ISBN 0-87116-074-9

MANUFACTURED IN THE UNITED STATES OF AMERICA

CONTENTS

INTRODUCTION

Years and years ago, when I was earning my living exclusively as a free-lance magazine writer, a kind but not gentle friend grabbed me by the scruff of the neck and dragged me into the book business. I squawked in protest all the way. I didn't want to write books. Books were too long. They looked too difficult. The pay was too uncertain. Please, please, I begged, let me go back to the friendly world of magazines.

You may be going through a somewhat similar experience right now. You've observed the great floods of nonfiction books that are being sold. You've heard, perhaps, that there is money to be made by writing such books and that beginners are welcome. Possibly you have written some magazine articles in the past or possibly you have never written anything for sale and publication, but in either case you enjoy tinkering with words and you feel you are basically capable of turning out a good book. Yet the prospect of starting any such project frightens you, as it did me. The idea of researching, planning, organizing, writing and selling such a huge bundle of words looks absolutely overwhelming.

Well, I can tell you honestly that, like any new experience, writing a book looks considerably harder than it really is. It looks more scary to those who haven't tried it than to those who have. I feel today like a man who signed up for a course in skiing, expecting to be laughed at, to feel ridiculously clumsy and perhaps to end with a broken leg. My fears were unreasonable. I came down the slope in fairly good order, not with perfect grace but at least upright. Nobody laughed at me, and I walked away on two whole legs. Today, with the advantage of hindsight, I can ask myself why I put off that first attempt so long.

It is obvious that you harbor some kind of yearning to write a book. That is why you picked up this one, which, I hope, will help you translate that yearning into action. By the time you reach the end of this book, if I have done my job properly, you should be thinking to yourself, "Why, yes, it *can* be done." It can indeed.

It matters little if you have never written a book before. It matters little, indeed, if you have never before earned a dime from any type of writing. The basic equipment you need is a fondness for words, a cleverness with them, an enjoyment of the writing process. I will assume you have this equipment, for it is unlikely anybody without it would be taking the time to read this book. Beyond this, you need only some knowledge of nonfiction book techniques, plus the courage to make your first attempt.

The basic equipment — the general state of being at home with paper and typewriter — is hard to come by. You have been struggling to achieve it, as we all have, since the early grades in school. It took years to win the degree of ease with language that you command today. But the other two elements — the techniques, the courage — can be had much more quickly.

I believe you will have them both when you have reached the last page of this book.

MAX GUNTHER

WRITING AND SELLING A
NONFICTION BOOK

I

WHAT MAKES A GOOD NONFICTION BOOK IDEA?

"You don't have to be anybody very special to make big money with a nonfiction book," an editor once grumbled to me. "You don't even have to know how to write. All you really need is a catchy idea."

The editor exaggerated, of course — and rather grossly, at that. He was feeling bitter that day. Jealousy had temporarily fogged his normally clear judgment. He was talking specifically about the huge success being enjoyed by a competing publisher with a somewhat clumsily written, but astoundingly popular, book having to do with sex.

In a little while, he came back to his senses and admitted that, yes, a nonfiction book must have more substance to it than a mere catchy idea. In general and in the long run, soundly researched and carefully written nonfiction books sell better than those which are just flashy ideas with nothing between the covers. On the other hand, I felt obliged to admit to the editor that there was a nugget of truth in the exaggerated statement he had made — and you, as a beginner, can profit by pondering this truth.

The idea of a book is indeed important, enormously so. If you want to write and sell a nonfiction book, the absolutely essential first step is to develop a good idea. This good idea will convince a book editor that he should read your manuscript in the first place, and obviously this must happen be-

3

fore anything else can happen. Similarly, if all goes well and the book is eventually published, that same good idea will convince people they should at least think about buying it — should at least pick up a copy in a bookstore, scan what's said on the jacket, glance at the table of contents. The final fate of the book will of course depend on many, many factors, but without a good idea the book will never be born at all.

There is another interesting fact about book ideas that you ought to consider: *A beginner is just as likely to have a good idea as is a veteran writer, and publishers know it.* The sex book my editor friend was grousing about had, in fact, been written by a man who had never attempted a book before. He was an absolute beginner — simply a man into whose head, one bright day, had popped a perfectly glorious book idea. Book editors spend a lot of their time trying to find people to write books, and they approach beginners almost as often as established professionals. They approach, for instance, people who chance to have been involved in notable news events. After the fatal rioting at Attica Prison in New York in 1971, for instance, publishers eagerly sought out potential authors of books directly or peripherally relevant to the subject. Convicts, prison guards, and others who had never even written magazine articles before suddenly found themselves signing juicy book contracts.

The chances that you will be personally involved in a news event of that magnitude are, of course, not great. But whoever you are, wherever you are, it is nearly certain that you are now involved or can become involved in something people will want to read about. A good book idea may be just a few thoughts away.

It may not be a big-news book, and you definitely should not look forward to its being a best seller — for nobody knows why best sellers happen; they just do, and it's impossible to predict in advance how any given book will fare. Your book may be a quiet and modest one. It may be a textbook dealing with your hobby or profession, or a book drawn from your life as a factory worker or housewife or accountant. You don't have to shoot for best-sellerdom. An idea can be small and quiet, yet still be good.

Very well. Just what is a good book idea?

There are, I believe, eight distinct qualities that separate good ideas from unsalable ones. Possibly other nonfiction book writers would add to my list of eight; possibly still others would say not all of the eight are as important as I think. I am virtually certain, however, that most nonfictioneers would agree my list is basically sound and incorporates most of what's important. I speak as a man who has seen many book ideas reach a profitable status in the bookstores — and, make no mistake about this, has seen a vastly larger number of ideas go nowhere. All my salable ideas have incorporated all eight of the elements I am going to list below. All my abortive ideas have lacked at least one, usually more, of the eight.

1. *A good book idea is sharply focused on a single, well-defined subject.* Its boundaries are clearly visible. It is easily grasped as a single idea, rather than as a loose collection of facts about this or that. *It can be explained and its boundaries defined in one sentence.*

Let me give you an illustration from my own experience. Some time in 1970 I conceived the idea of writing a book about people who win consistently in the stock market. I was going to call it *The Winners*, or something like that. My notion was to interview a gaggle of people and in the book present their explanations of their methods for beating the market — one person and one method per chapter.

I submitted the idea to my regular publisher, and when the editors there turned it down, to others. No go. Everybody said the idea was too vague, too broad. How would I limit the number of interviewees? What excuse could I give the book's readers for including one stock-trading approach but excluding others, of which there are several hundred at least? No, the idea lacked focus, the feeling of *singleness*. Instead of feeling like a hard, dense nugget, as every good idea does, it felt something like a double handful of marshmallows.

I shrugged and turned to other projects. Then, while idly looking through magazines one day at my local stationery store, I happened to notice an astrology annual with a big purple announcement on the cover: "Special! Stock Market Forecast for 1970-75!"

I stared at that purple print, suddenly dizzy with delight. I thought, this is it! The book idea of the century! A book on the use of astrology in the stock market!

But that is only what I thought.

2. *A good idea is what editors call "rich," as opposed to "thin."* That is, although the idea is sharply focused on a single subject, it still contains within its boundaries enough good, solid material to fill a book without padding or repetition.

My market-astrology idea was — as I saw for myself when I calmed down — much too thin. To write an entire book about Wall Street astrologers would be nearly impossible without boring the reader (and no doubt the author) halfway through. There are dozens, even hundreds, of astrologers operating in and around the market, but their approaches are all essentially similar. Perhaps it would be possible to find three or four who are diverse enough to be worth lining up side-by-side in a book. But how about Chapters Five through Ten? How would I fill them? With what?

Sadly, I abandoned the idea. Over the next several weeks, the two dead ideas — *The Winners* and the astrologers — kept drifting in and out of my head at odd moments. I thought, there *must* be a good idea in this area somewhere.

It came to me on an airplane heading for Washington, D.C. I noticed two things almost simultaneously. The stewardess wore a necklace bearing an astrological symbol; and two college girls in front of me were telling each other's fortunes with a deck of Tarot cards. And at last I saw the shape of this book that had had so much trouble getting born: It would be a book about people who had won by using occult and mystical approaches to the stock market — including, but not limited to, astrologers.

It had the focus demanded by Rule 1. And the richness demanded by Rule 2. It became *Wall Street and Witchcraft,* published in 1971 (Geis), one of the more profitable projects I've ever had the good luck to tackle.

3. *The idea must have inherent interest and value for the reader.* To put it another way, your embryo book should not only be "about"; it should also be "for the purpose of." Before you write a word, before you even suggest the idea to a publisher, you must be able to see with perfect clarity what value the reader will derive from the book, what needs of his you will be trying to satisfy, what nerves of his you will touch or what aches you will soothe.

A book "about" your camping trip through the Rocky Mountains might be a perfectly good book. But the idea is not salable — by you to the publisher or by the publisher to the readers — until you and the publisher both know very precisely why you are asking anybody to spend his valuable time reading these x-thousand words.

Merely to say, "because it's interesting," is not precise enough. You must offer more specific reasons. You might feel, for example, that your camping-trip book is educational, that other camping families reading the book will avoid your mistakes and so enjoy themselves more. Very well; that is a good reason for writing the book, and it will heavily influence the way in which you write it. Or you might feel the book has something important to say about ecology and the preservation of wilderness areas. That is a different reason and will generate a different book.

The point is that this reason must exist, must be known to you right at the beginning, must be seen clearly as a component of the idea. Without this component, the idea will be too fuzzy. You won't visualize the book well enough to write it successfully, and the editor won't visualize it well enough to buy it.

4. *An editor must be able to visualize clearly the readership of the book.* In part, this is necessary because an editor, before betting his time and his company's money on the book, must know where he can advertise the book, to whom, how many potential readers there are, and so on. It is also necessary for the writer himself to visualize the readers. You *must* know, in the very beginning, whom you'll be writing to. Without this knowledge your idea hangs in a kind of limbo. It needs to be connected to the ultimate consumers.

Often this knowledge of the readership follows naturally when, in obedience to Rule 3, you figure out why anybody would want to read your book. For instance, if your hypothetical camping book were designed mainly to give practical instruction, then obviously the bulk of your readers would be camping enthusiasts. But sometimes you must think a little longer to see the readers clearly.

In the case of *Wall Street and Witchcraft*, I first thought I would be writing to people with a curiosity about the so-called "unknown" — the kind of reader who buys books about ghosts and amazing prophecies. But then I thought, no, the book might also attract ordinary stock speculators who have been having a hard time in the recent bear markets. They might feel that, since rational forecasting techniques haven't helped them much, they might want to try or at least look into irrational or occult techniques. Or their wives, half in jest, might give them the book as a gift. This thought nudged the idea into a whole new shape and of course played a large role in the shaping of the book itself.

I had to think all this through at the very start. The idea was not whole until I had done so.

5. *The idea must have a quality of immediacy.* It must have relevance to the lives people are living today. There must exist some felt or stated excuse for publishing it now, rather than last decade or next. As a Doubleday editor once remarked to me, "Even if it's a history book, it has to be written from this year's viewpoint, not last year's."

My Wall Street book was decidedly influenced by the fact that it was written for publication in 1971. We had just lived through a two-year economic slump and stock-market dive, and these unhappy facts circulated in the very bloodstream of my book. If I had written it in 1968, it would have been a different book, with a different outlook, probably a gayer tone. The current economic situation, in fact, helped me decide how to answer the question posed by Rule 3 — why anybody would want to read what I planned to write.

Before you submit any idea to an editor, you must be prepared to answer his question, "Why now?" In fact you must answer it for him within the body of the idea. If you don't, he will think, "Well, next year will be soon enough." And, as he is keenly aware, potential readers will think the same.

6. *There must be a quality of "differentness" in the idea.* That is, the proposed book must sound to the editor, and later to the potential buyers, as though it will be different from other currently available books on the same or related subjects.

With some ideas this requirement is easily satisfied. My Wall Street idea was different simply because, as far as the publisher or I knew, nobody had ever tackled this offbeat subject in book form before.

But suppose you're proposing to write a textbook about your hobby — let's say coin collecting. There are a number of coin-collecting textbooks and catalogues currently on the market. Most of them chalk up steady, though not spectacular, sales. There is no reason why a publisher devoted to this type of book wouldn't want to publish another. But he must be convinced in advance that the proposed new book will be different in some substantial way from the others — that it will contain more or newer information, for example, or that it will be cross-indexed in some new and useful way, or that it will appeal more strongly than the others to beginning hobbyists.

This quality of differentness becomes a built-in part of the idea. You aren't just writing "a coin-collecting textbook." You are writing a "textbook that is new because. . . ."

7. *The writer's emotional and stylistic approach to the subject matter must be built into the idea.* That is, you must know, before you talk to any editor and before you start to write, precisely how you feel about the subject and how you want the reader to feel.

My Wall Street idea was not whole without this element. I had to know — and so did the publisher — how I was going to treat the occultists and mystics I interviewed. Would the book's tone of voice be dead serious? Exhortative, urging the readers to go mystical? Humorous? Fun-poking? Tongue-in-cheek? It was absolutely essential that I answer these questions before talking to my editors.

My answer was colored partly by my thoughts arising from Rules 3, 4 and 5: the questions of who would read the book, why, and why now. I decided my tone of voice would be reportorial, skeptical but open-minded. I would approach my occultists in the full and repeatedly stated knowledge that they might be kidding me or themselves, but my attitude toward them would be on the whole fond and friendly. Without this early thinking, my idea would have lacked an essential element of color.

8. *The proposed book must sound possible.* The editor, reading or listening to the suggested idea, must be able to think, "Yes, this writer is capable of turning out this book."

There are many potential book ideas that could easily satisfy all seven of the other rules but flunk out on this one. To take an extreme example, almost any publisher in the world would like to buy rights to a book entitled *My Trip to Mars*. It is conceivable that an astronaut will some day write this book. But you or I, if we were to suggest it, would simply not be able to satisfy the eighth requirement.

For a less extreme example, consider the war in Vietnam. This war has been, and will perhaps continue to be, a source of many books. But if you or I were to suggest such a book the editor would have some questions to ask. "Why *you?* Can *you* get to Vietnam? Do *you* have any high-placed contacts in Washington?" And so on.

It really comes down to an aura of confidence surrounding the idea. You must be confident of your own ability to produce the proposed book, either because you're already familiar with the subject or because you can perceive with clarity the research routes you will take. A good editor will very quickly sense the presence or absence of this confidence. He will not buy, and you should never propose, an impossible book.

II

TYPES OF NONFICTION BOOKS

Classifying books into types is something like classifying people. Carried too far, it can lead to serious difficulties. Each book, like each man and woman, is unique. There is no other precisely like it. The moment you set up a list of categories and try to fit all the world's books into those categories, problems arise. A given book might seem to belong in several categories at once, and the category in which it ends up may depend on the viewpoint of the individual reader. Another book may not fit comfortably into any category at all. Still another might appear to drift through the categories as times and attitudes change.

But classifications can be useful if they are approached with a strong awareness that the categories can't be exact, and that the process of breaking a group of things down into component parts depends partly on subjective judgment. The classification called "books" — roughly divided into two sub-classes, fiction and nonfiction — is so enormous and so staggeringly diverse that we must break it down further, into perceived types, to make sense out of it.

We are dealing, of course, with nonfiction books. Let's see what common types of nonfiction books there are.

The list which follows lays no claim to completeness. It includes the broad categories of nonfiction books that publishers most often seek. The books are not classified by sub-

12

ject matter, as in a library, but by structure and general approach to subject matter. The list may help you make some preliminary decisions about the kind of book you want to write, and may get you started in the process of generating ideas.

Adult how-to. Such a book offers instruction in a certain field of expertise and is written by an author who can claim to be an authority on the subject.

Everybody is an authority on something, and publishers eternally seek authoritative books in a huge variety of subjects. Sports, hobbies, arts and crafts, careers, aspects of business, spare-time moneymaking ventures: All are fields where good how-to books are welcomed. How-to books are among the easiest for a beginner to write and sell, for in general such a book represents less of a gamble for the publisher than many other kinds of book. If the beginner's basic idea is sound, his chances of getting a hearing from a publisher are excellent.

Adult how-to books differ from the textbooks used in schools and colleges. Those are almost all written by people with specific academic credentials. Unless you are in the education profession yourself, your chances of selling a school or college textbook are not good.

The mere fact that there are already other adult how-to books in your field need not discourage you from trying another. As we have seen, two of the qualities that make a good book idea are *immediacy* and *differentness.* There is no requirement that the idea be "first of the breed." As an example, consider the stock market. New books in this field appear every year, but publishers still want more, and readers keep buying them.

General descriptive book. This kind of book is related to the *adult how-to,* but it lacks the direct how-to approach.

Books of this type strive mainly to satisfy readers' curiosity about a particular subject, without actually giving instruction.

A book of this kind might explain how the stock market works, or it might explain or describe anything about which the writer thinks people (potential readers) may be curious. It might describe life and politics in a foreign country — modern China, for example. At this point in history, such a book would have the quality of immediacy, for the American public at the moment is highly curious about what goes on inside that mysterious and influential country. Or such a descriptive book might deal with the behind-the-scenes maneuverings of a specific Presidential election campaign.

Descriptive books are among the most difficult to sell, for it is often hard to state clearly why anyone would care to read the book. Merely to say, "because it is interesting," is not enough. The subject may interest you, but the publisher must be convinced that it will also interest a large reading public.

This quality of interest may come not only from the subject matter, but also from the author's emotional and stylistic approach. Let's turn back to the stock market as a subject area, for example. We've noted that how-to books on the market have been selling well throughout the century. These books attract readers by promising to show them how to get rich. But general descriptive books about the stock market are vastly harder to sell — and, as a result, they appear in the bookstores much less often. A recent one was *The Money Game,* by a man writing under the pseudonym of Adam Smith. He sold his book to the publisher, and the publisher sold it to large numbers of readers, mainly by satisfying the seventh requirement — style — in an attractive way. Smith's humorous, cynical, erudite style drew his readers to the book.

Alarmer or exposé. This is the kind of book that dramatically points out something the author believes to be wrong. Recent books in this category have grumbled about such subjects as prison conditions, destruction of the environment, race relations, the social and economic status of women, and the conduct of U.S. foreign affairs.

Sound ideas in this category are welcomed at publishing houses, for such books have sometimes sold astoundingly well. Betty Friedan's alarmer, *The Feminine Mystique,* for instance, is generally acknowledged to have been a major factor in the birth of the women's liberation movement. It became a bible of the movement and is still being sold in bookstores today, years after its original publication. Very few alarmers — in fact, very few books of any kind — sell that well, of course. But the dream of repeating such success keeps publishers alert for good new alarmers.

For a beginner, one of the main hurdles to jump in selling an alarmer is that the proposed book must sound *possible.* You may believe you have some excellent ideas for reducing public school costs and property taxes, for example, and you may believe you can turn out a hot alarmer on the topic. But an editor will say, "Why *you?* I'd feel safer buying this idea from an established writer."

The beginner's answer must be that he knows the field better than any other writer the editor could reasonably hope to find — that he knows it from top to bottom. For this reason, it is better for a beginner to pick a narrowly limited topic rather than a broad one. *The Feminine Mystique* dealt with an extremely broad topic: the social and economic experience of being a woman. Millions of other women besides Betty Friedan could conceivably have written a book on the subject. But it is unlikely that a beginner, suggesting the idea to a publisher, would have made a sale. Betty Friedan was able to sell the idea because she was an established writer. A beginner would have found it hard to prove that *she* knew more about the subject than Betty Friedan or any other woman.

A beginner, competing with established professionals, must pick an alarmer topic in which the pros lack expert knowledge. Richard Ney did this in 1970, for instance. Although he had never written a book before, he sold an alarmer called *The Wall Street Jungle,* in which he criticized the specialists who make markets in securities on the stock exchanges. Ney could sell the book because he was an expert in this narrowly defined subject. Few established writers, if any, could have matched his thorough, inside knowledge. The book was among the more successful alarmers of that year.

Your alarmer, should you want to write one, can be drawn from your own experience. If you work in a government bureau, for example, you may be in a position to write an alarmer dealing with wasteful spending of taxpayers' money. If you work in a retail store, perhaps your alarmer could deal with fraudulent pricing practices. If your own experience doesn't seem to yield any such topic, you can develop one through independent research in some field where you think criticism is called for. The point is that by the time you carry your idea to an editor, you must be prepared to satisfy him that you know more about this subject — and therefore can write a better-documented book — than an established writer.

Microcosmic adventure narrative. In this type of book, by telling the detailed story of an adventure that happened to you or others, you illuminate some subject about which people are curious or worried. This adventure narrative becomes what editors sometimes like to call a "microcosm." It focuses narrowly on a relatively small group of people in a specific situation, but it is taken to be typical or illustrative of many such situations or of a larger problem.

Such a narrative can be *current* or *historical.* For example:

In a *current* narrative, you might tell the story of a group of citizens who fought to get industrial wastes cleaned out of a certain stretch of river. These people, their battle, their opponents, their stretch of river would be the microcosm. You would focus down on it, telling their story in high detail. But your story, though tightly limited, would illuminate the problems and prospects of ecology as a whole. You would become something like a biologist who, focusing on a single cell through his microscope, draws conclusions about the entire body.

An *historical* narrative, as the name implies, would focus similarly on something that happened in the past — an adventure that had some relevance to the problems or curiosities of today. As an example, I once proposed to write a book about Jack the Ripper, perhaps history's most famous criminal. He lived in nineteenth-century London and he was never caught. The fact that he was never caught left the book without a clearly definable ending, so after arguing with editors for a while I abandoned the idea. The book didn't sound *possible.* I showed the editors that I could get to London and see Scotland Yard's files, but I failed to show that those files would yield what the book needed. Yet the basic premise seemed sound to me and the editors alike. The book could have had something to say about violence in certain types of societies and about people's varied reactions to it.

Delving into more recent history, I've had it in mind for years to write an adventure narrative dealing with the Hartford (Connecticut) circus fire of 1944. This fire took a huge toll of lives and was famous in its day. All the bodies were identified except that of one little girl. Nobody ever came forward to claim her. One Hartford police officer made it his business to find out who she was and why nobody wanted her, and he spent eighteen years on the trail. He ended with a theory, though not with positive proof. My book, if I ever write it, will be the year-by-year story of this cop and his developing love for a loveless little girl. The book won't illuminate the kinds of problems that make daily newspaper headlines. Instead it will talk about love and non-love, altruism and selfishness.

Friends occasionally ask me why I don't stop talking about this book and write it. I always answer that I'm too busy. The real reason is that I am scared of the idea. I suspect I may be the wrong kind of writer for that kind of book. A writer must coldly assess his own strengths and weaknesses — and that is a subject we'll consider in a later chapter.

Biography or ghosted autobiography. The book tells the life story of a man or woman, either in the subject's own words (first person) or in yours (third person).

As a general rule, the biographies or ghostwritten autobiographies of the very famous who are still living — *current* biographies — are written by established professionals. It would be hard for a beginner to break into the lucrative business of writing, for example, the life stories of currently popular movie stars. Not impossible, but hard.

Such a book might be conceived by the writer himself. He approaches the movie star and suggests that he and the star collaborate on a biography, on the basis of some equitable split of the money. If the star agrees, the writer then approaches a publisher with the idea. Unless the writer is established, with other published books to his credit, it is rather unlikely the star would go along with such a deal.

Alternately, the star might conceive the book. The star writes an autobiography and submits it to a publisher. The publisher, attracted by the star's name and fame, believes the book will sell tolerably well. But the star isn't much of a writer, so the publisher must go out and find somebody to rework the book. Obviously, the publisher will hire a pro for this job, not an unknown beginner.

But these facts don't freeze the beginner entirely out of the current biography business. You might get your foot in the door by writing the biography of someone semi-famous. Perhaps, at some time in your life, your path has crossed that of a political figure or entertainer or business leader or consumer activist in your state. You have some casual acquaintanceship with this semi-famous person — or you have a friend who has a friend who will approach him for you. The semi-famous person, not having made the national big time yet, may be intrigued by the idea of publishing a biography and thus increasing his exposure. He may be happy to talk to you about it — may indeed be flattered that somebody is finally paying attention to him. He may even be so eager for publicity that he will agree to subsidize the book in some fashion. Business leaders, or their companies, often subsidize biographies by making direct cash payments to publishers or by contracting to buy a certain number of the books when published. Either way, this reduces the publisher's risk and makes it easier for you to sell the idea. Many a beginner has been launched by this route.

An equally fertile field for the beginner is that of *historical* biographies. You find some influential figure from the past, somebody whose life seems to have some relevance to the fears and hopes of people today. It need not be a great statesman or military hero or king or queen. It might be, indeed, someone rather obscure — someone whose name people recognize but vaguely, or whose life was intertwined with a recognized historical event but whose name is hardly known at all.

In this latter sub-category, one book that has long stayed in my mind is *The Reason Why*, by Cecil Woodham-Smith. The book deals with the lives of three men who were responsible for the famous charge of the Light Brigade during the Crimean War. By analyzing these men's lives and the times in which they lived, the author shows how one of history's most ill-advised and tragic military ventures could happen.

(Woodham-Smith, incidentally, also wrote an excellent book
about a much better-known historical personality, Florence
Nightingale.)

An historical biography can be written either for adult
readers, as Woodham-Smith's are, or for young people. Biographies of the famous are in particularly great demand
in upper grades and high schools, and in this field it need not
matter that several other biographies of the same person already exist. If you can show that your proposed biography
of President Roosevelt or Queen Victoria offers some fresh
and relevant insights for a young audience *this* year, *this*
decade, the chances that a publisher will listen to you are
good.

Your proposed book must also sound possible. Before approaching an editor with a proposed historical biography —
particularly in the case of a little-known figure such as those
in *The Reason Why* — you must be prepared to show that
you can find enough data on this person to build a book. You
must do a certain amount of library research before an editor
will listen to you.

Anthology. Articles on a certain well-defined subject,
drawn from magazines or other sources, are gathered together to form a book. The gatherer, or writer-editor, com-
poses introductory and other material, and this material becomes the glue that holds the articles together.

Generally, this isn't a fertile field for beginners. Nine
times out of ten, anthology ideas are conceived by editors at
publishing houses. Having decided to publish an anthology
on a certain subject, the editor phones a writer with whom
he has worked in the past, or whose work he has read and
admired. The writer then collects the articles, makes the
necessary deals with the articles' copyright owners, and glues
the book together.

Building an anthology is a pleasant change of pace for

the nonfiction book writer. I recently built one for Playboy Press — *The Very, Very Rich and How They Got That Way* — and though I resisted the assignment in the beginning, I ended by enjoying it thoroughly. I mention this because it is something for you to bear in mind for the future. Once you have published your first nonfiction book, you become a potential candidate for anthology work in the field in which you have demonstrated expertise.

These are the major nonfiction book categories in which publishers today are seeking writers. There are other, smaller categories I haven't mentioned, and of course any one of the categories can be divided into dozens or even hundreds of sub-categories. But perhaps, after this brief stroll along the bookstore shelves, you are beginning to form some thoughts about the kind of nonfiction book you want to write.

Don't fret if your ideas at the moment seem vague, fuzzy, amorphous. Every nonfiction writer carries dozens of half-formed book ideas in his head at once. You need only let them mature at their own pace. You keep your eyes and ears open, read your newspapers every day, talk, listen, brood. Eventually, one of your ideas will begin to take on a more detailed form and will begin to stand out starkly from the others. Then you will know what category it falls in, what kind of book it will be, how you are going to handle it. A book idea will have been born.

Your next problem will be to sell it.

III

The Query Letter: Pre-Selling Your Book

One of the more pleasant features of the nonfiction book field is that, to a large degree, the books are sold before they are written.

This is an enormous benefit for the writer. It means that he doesn't have to gamble months' or years' time on a book, only to discover in the end, perhaps, that the book is unsalable. Instead, he risks his time in small increments. He proceeds in stages, like a swimmer testing the water temperature with his toe before he commits himself to total immersion. If the risk begins to look too large in the early stages, the writer can back off and abandon the project without having lost a great deal of time.

There are three major stages in the selling of a nonfiction book:

1. *The initial query.* Most often this takes the form of a brief query letter. It can be a phone call if you have dealt with the publisher before and know him well. It could also be done with a phone call if you had a particularly compelling, hot, newsy topic to discuss — if, for example, you had somehow nailed down an agreement to ghostwrite a U. S. President's autobiography. But such cases are extremely rare. In general, a query letter rather than a phone call is the beginner's best bet. If an editor receives a phone call from

somebody he never heard of before, he is more likely to be irritated than interested.

If you can't find any publishers to express interest in your book idea on the basis of your initial query, you may want to abandon the book. You have lost only a little time and a little postage. But if you find an editor who says, "Yes, tell me more," you proceed to the second stage of selling. The editor himself, in fact, will almost certainly ask you to take this second step:

2. *Outline and sample chapters.* You expand on what you have said in the query letter, and you write an outline and some chapters (two or three are usually enough) to demonstrate your command of the language, your grip on the research, your tone and approach to the material.

In brief, by your performance in this second stage, you will either satisfy the editor that the book is promising and that he should encourage you to finish it — or you will convince him that the idea isn't as good as he originally thought. If your outline reinforces his original hopes, he may now commit his time and some of his company's money by offering you a book contract. Or he may not go that far: he may ask to see still more chapters. But in either case, he has shown that he is as eager as you to see the book succeed, and he will work with you to help you pull it off.

3. *The finished book.* Having come through the first two stages with your book idea still alive, you can now go ahead and write the book with minimal risk. The editor may not have guaranteed to buy it and publish it, but at least you have the comforting knowledge that your idea is basically a sound one. Your chances of seeing it in print, at this point, are good.

Now let's turn back to the first stage and see how an effective initial query letter is written. As an example, here is a very brief query I wrote in 1970. It was the opening move in the process of selling the book that was eventually entitled *Wall Street and Witchcraft*:

Dear —:
How would you like to publish a book about occult and mystical approaches to the stock market?

As far as I can find out, no book on precisely this subject has ever been written. Not in recent times, anyhow. It's an intriguing subject for a couple of reasons. Books on the stock market are selling well right now, and so are books on the occult. This would be a book on both. The time seems ripe. If I bring it off right, people could read it either for entertainment or for instruction. The buyers would presumably be stock-market buffs or those who are curious about the occult. I can also see the wife of a market player giving it to her husband for Christmas — maybe in seriousness, maybe as a gag.

As I envision it, the book would be composed mainly of narrative-style case histories. I'd pick one or two market mystics in each of perhaps a dozen categories: astrology, dream interpretation, Tarot cards, numerology, ESP and so on. I'd tell their stories, with strong emphasis on the amounts of money they made and how they made it. At the end of each narrative section, I'd give the reader some instructions for using this particular type of approach himself. The tone would be humorous but friendly, skeptical but not sarcastic.

Finding all these mystics will present some problems, of course. There are many people around who *say* they've beaten the market by occult means, but when you ask them to prove it, their lovely stories evaporate. I plan to insist on seeing documentation or other hard evidence, and this will obviously narrow the field. But the chances seem excellent that I can come up with, say, fifteen good, hard, documented stories. For instance, I've already contacted a man named David Williams, who believes the market is influenced by sunspots and who has steadily doubled his money every three years. He has told me about another successful occult market player, an astrologer, who may earn a place in the book. I've also talked to brokers in and around Wall Street, and some have told me about mystical-type customers of theirs whom I can track down. With luck, each man or woman I talk to will lead me to others.

How does this sound to you? Would you like to see some chapters and a more complete outline?

A few days after I mailed this letter, the editor replied: "Dear Max: Eureka! . . ."

My letter was not the most compelling ever written, but it did obey what I consider the major rules of an effective query.

The first rule is to keep the query brief. Two single-spaced typewritten pages are almost always enough. This letter is basically a device for introducing yourself, getting attention for your idea and sounding out editorial opinion. Unlike the outline that you will write later, it is not intended to describe the book's architecture in detail. The editors who read it will appreciate its brevity. A good idea will leap up at them even from a very short note, while no tonnage of words will make an unattractive idea sound any better.

The second rule is to keep it informal, friendly, lively. Since this is your first contact with the editors, it is essential that you show them, in the very beginning, that you are at home with the language. If your letter is stiff and formal, this will make the editors pessimistic right away. It will make them think you are uncomfortable with your typewriter. Avoid business-letter jargon. Avoid dumb phrases like, "In reference to the above matter . . ." or "Trusting this matter will receive your prompt attention . . ." Instead, talk English. Use contractions liberally — "I've" instead of "I have." Don't strain too far in the opposite direction and overload your letter with slang; just talk naturally, as though you were sitting with the editors over a cup of coffee.

The third rule is to give an editor all the data he needs to make an intelligent preliminary decision about your idea — and to decide that he wants to hear more. If you do it right (always assuming your idea is basically sound, of course), he will look up from the letter with a sudden feeling of hope, what one editor friend of mine calls "the feeling of *hey, maybe* . . ." Every editor recognizes this exhilarating feeling and combs eagerly through his mail each day in the hope he will find something to bring the feeling on. He doesn't find this something every day, nor even every month. Your competition is not that formidable. If your idea and your query letter are good, you will get your hearing.

To fulfill this third rule, your letter should contain seven elements. They seem to flow most logically in this order for me, though you may find a different order more comfortable:

1. If you are unknown to the publishing house — you have addressed your letter simply to "The Editors" or "Managing Editor" — start right off by saying who you are and why you should be considered a potential book writer. I didn't need to do this in my *Wall Street* query, for this was to be the fifth book I had written for that company. If you are a beginner, you can open your letter something like this:

Dear Sir:
    I'm a teacher at XYZ School. Though I've never written a book for publication before, I've been doing some research into what I think is an unusually intriguing subject. I think it's a book. May I tell you about it?

2. Next, state the basic idea of your book in its briefest possible form — preferably in a single sentence. I did this in the first paragraph of my *Wall Street* query. Every good nonfiction book idea is capable of being stated this briefly; if it can't be so stated, it is probably too diffuse.

Don't try to embellish this single-sentence statement at this point in your letter. The idea is to make the editor see the book *whole,* to plant the essential idea in his mind and let it churn around there for a while.

3. Tell the editor why your proposed book will be different from others, if any, on the same general subject. In my *Wall Street* query, this was easy to do: There were no recently

published books on the subject, as far as the publisher or I knew. I took care to state this fact in my query. If you are tackling a frequently-covered subject, state the facts that make your book new and fresh. For example: "The last biography of Abraham Lincoln for young people was published in 19—. My book will take a fresh look at the subject, in light of the vast social changes that have taken place in this country since then . . ." Or: "My research has turned up some surprising facts that seem to throw a whole new light on the subject. Briefly, the facts are that . . ."

4. Say who you think the potential readers will be and why they will want to buy the book. In effect, you are helping the editor visualize how he might advertise the book if he were to publish it.

5. Provide a few more details about the structure and character of the proposed book. In effect, what you are now doing is expanding on your single-sentence statement of the book's basic idea. I took care of this element in the third paragraph of my *Wall Street* query, the paragraph beginning "As I envision it . . ." This paragraph helps the editor envision how the book will be built, helps him hear its tone of voice.

It is likely the editor will have some comments to make on this fifth element of your letter, if he decides to encourage you further. He may suggest changes in structure, approach, tone. This happened to me with the *Wall Street* book; the final structure was quite different from what I had originally proposed. No matter: It is important that you have thought about these factors before making your initial sales pitch. You must show the editor that you have done more than superficial thinking about your planned project.

6. Give the editor some idea of the factual bricks and mortar with which your book will be built. You must convince

him that you know how you're going to do your research, that the needed sources will be available to you, that you have thought through the possible problems of getting to these sources. Note that, in the fourth paragraph of my query, I carefully tell the editor that I've already done some preliminary poking around. I tell him I am not merely guessing that the book is possible. I *know* it is possible because I've taken the time to do some exploring in the field.

You do not need to do a great deal of this exploratory research before writing an initial query. Two or three days' worth will almost always be enough. You might even get by with a few phone calls and a couple of hours in a library. But it is essential that you do enough preliminary digging to talk knowledgeably about your proposed sources. Otherwise, the editor will be left with a question about your competence to gather the needed factual material. You must convince him you know what research *is*.

If you are proposing a book about some field in which you are an authority — an adult how-to book on your hobby, for example — then you become, in effect, the main research source. In such a case, this sixth element of your initial query should be a brief sketch of your own competence in the field: "I've been in the rare-coin business for fifteen years and in that time have corresponded with collectors all over the world . . ." Or, if you're proposing a personal-adventure narrative: "I personally knew most of the key participants in the rioting . . ."

7. Finally, offer to send the editor a more complete outline and some sample chapters, with no obligation on his part. This will show him that your approach is professional, that you have enough faith in your idea and your writing ability to gamble a little more time on them. If your letter conveys the impression that you expect the editor to offer you a juicy contract right away, that will mark you as an amateur.

What the editor *will* offer you, if he likes what you have said, is encouragement. At this point, you cannot reasonably ask for more. More, if it comes, will come later.

Certainly it is true that an occasional amateur sells a book without writing a good query or a good outline. But this is usually a case of sheer, blind luck. If you happened to be standing on the spot when the first bona fide visitors from outer space landed on earth, you would have a potential blockbuster of a book. You wouldn't need to write any queries or outlines. Editors would query *you*.

But blockbuster books are very, very rare. For the average nonfiction writer — for you, for me — it is better to depend on skill than on luck. You can cultivate skill. Nobody has ever discovered a way to cultivate luck.

IV

THE OUTLINE AND SAMPLE CHAPTERS

Many nonfiction writers feel the task of outlining a book is the hardest part of the entire process — harder, in its way, than writing the book itself. I cannot argue. It *is* hard.

The main difficulty is that you are being forced to visualize a book that may not yet be completely formed in your mind. The research is not yet complete — indeed, is perhaps barely begun. You cannot know, at this stage, precisely where the research will lead or how its unknowable course will influence the final book. You cannot know what new thoughts will drift into your head during the long months of researching and writing, what new intellectual doors will open, what doors that now seem open will slam shut in your face. It may seem to you, as you sit down to write your outline, that you really know very little about this book you are planning to write.

Hard indeed! Some of the most memorably painful days in my writing career have been those in which I worked on outlines. No unwritten book ever *wants* to be outlined.

But take heart. There is something you should know.

An outline is not a rigid, formal contract between you and your book, nor between you and your publisher. It is a sort of promise, yes — but only sort of. It contains hope as well as promise. When you write an outline, you are saying, in effect, "This is how I hope the book will turn out, but I can't guarantee every detail."

Book editors are fully aware of the difficulties inherent in outlines. No editor will attempt to hold you to the letter of an outline, like a lawyer nitpicking about fine print in a contract. No editor will object if your book, when finished, wanders down pathways not mentioned in your outline — or, conversely, fails to cover a certain piece of ground the outline said would be covered. Your reasons for making such changes of plan must be good reasons, of course, and obviously the book itself must be good. But the mere fact that you have strayed from your original outline will not make anybody mad.

"I'd be silly to make an author follow an outline the way an engineer follows a blueprint," an editor at Playboy Press once told me. "Books aren't machines. They're more like people. They have to be allowed to develop in their own way, without unnecessary restrictions. If you try to force a book into a certain preconceived mold, you can sometimes damage it badly. You can even kill it."

He was referring specifically to a book on which I was working, *The Very, Very Rich and How They Got That Way.* The book was conceived as a collection of stories dealing with rich men such as Howard Hughes and Edwin Land, with special emphasis on the means by which each piled up his wealth. In my original outline, I had said I was going to cover seventeen of the very, very rich. But, halfway through my work on the book, I was coming up against the old truth about the best laid plans of mice and men. Some of the rich men I'd hoped to include would not cooperate with me. Others, it turned out, had lived less dramatic lives than I'd thought, and I no longer wanted to include them. In addition, my research had turned up several charmingly obscure rich men whom I now wanted to include, but who hadn't appeared anywhere in my outline.

Did it matter? Not at all. Despite these changes, the original broad concept of the book was still holding up beautifully. The fact that I strayed from my outline troubled nobody — not me, not the editors.

To give you a statistical picture of this phenomenon — a book willfully going its own way, stubbornly seeking freedom from the outline that is supposed to control it — here is how that original outline differed from the book that was finally published in the spring of 1972:

The outline proposed seventeen case studies. The book contains fifteen.

Of the seventeen men mentioned in the outline, ten appear in the book.

Of the fifteen men in the book, five had not appeared in the outline.

In the usual case, an outline is delivered to a publisher along with two or three sample chapters. This package is, in effect, the author's final sales pitch for the book — the first having been a query letter. The outline tells the editor something about the book's framework and the factual bricks and mortar with which it will be built, while the sample chapters tell him about the writing style, the emotional tone, the author's general competence to handle the material. The package enables the editor to decide whether or not he wants to see the book finished and published.

The sample chapters could be Chapter 3 and Chapter 8, or any others chosen at random, but in practice they are most often Chapters 1 and 2 and perhaps one other chapter. There are at least two sound reasons for this:

First, by starting at the beginning of the book, you automatically set the scene and tell the editor what the book is to be about. Your outline then simply picks up where your sample chapters left off, and you progress straight through to the end of the book. If your sample chapters are drawn instead from the middle of the book, you have some extra explaining and scene-setting to do at the start of the outline.

You waste time and you waste words, and unless you are an excellent outliner (which few nonfiction writers are, because they hate the task so much — and that includes me), the results may not be very effective.

Second, in the process of writing the first chapter or two, you will find your book growing steadily clearer in your mind. You will then be able to write a better outline than might otherwise have been possible.

Thus, though editors don't insist that every samples-and-outline package include Chapter 1, I would strongly urge you to approach the job this way. The process of producing the sales package now becomes reasonably straightforward. You go through several quite clearly defined steps, one step at a time.

You begin by spending a period of time — with some books it's a day or two, with others it's weeks — cogitating about your proposed book and trying to visualize its general shape. Some writers make great stacks of notes in this period. I'm not a note-maker, so I generally spend the period ambling around rather aimlessly. I write letters to friends, fix leaky faucets my wife has been nagging me about, overhaul my daughters' bikes. (Little girls' bikes always need repairing.) I go into town, mope about, gaze into store windows, drink a lot of coffee in diners, chat with policemen and anybody else who will stand still long enough. I gather a lot of information that is of no use to me whatever. I read obituaries and shipping announcements in newspapers. I watch soap operas on TV. And all the time I am trying to figure out what I want my book to say and in what order to say it.

Finally, the time is ripe for the second step, the process of writing Chapter 1. During the cogitating period, you have arrived at some large, vague, general decisions about your book. You know roughly what you want it to say; you know its boundaries; you have mentally arranged certain large blocks of subject matter in a logical and appealing order;

and you know what impact you want this book to have on the reader. Chapter 1 is to be your opening gambit. In this chapter, you must do three main things, and do them well:

1. Set the scene in terms of subject matter. That is, you tell what the book is about, define its boundaries.

2. Set the scene in terms of emotional effect. You let the reader know whether you want him to laugh, cry, be angry, be scared, have fun, grow rich — or whatever it may be. Immerse the reader in your style and your own feelings about the subject. By the time he reaches the end of Chapter 1, he should have a strong awareness of the book's personality.

3. Whet the reader's appetite so that he is drawn into the remainder of the book. Tell him why he should care; tantalize him, tease him a little by dropping hints about things you are going to tell him later on.

In the actual process of writing Chapter 1, you will inevitably find ideas suddenly starbursting in your head like Fourth-of-July rockets. The task of writing this opening chapter forces you to do some very precise thinking about your book, about where it will go and how it will get there. Without conscious effort on your part, the outline is constructing itself.

This is why I nearly always write the first chapter before trying to write a formal outline. While writing the chapter, I keep a large legal-sized notepad on the desk next to my typewriter stand. Almost every paragraph of Chapter 1, in the instant of being written, gives rise to at least one thought about subject matter that will or might or should appear later in the book — along with thoughts about where this piece of material should appear in relation to other pieces. I jot these thoughts down on the notepad as they arise, and in the process I try to arrive at a rough and preliminary chapter-by-chapter structure for my book.

I may cover as many as a dozen of those lined yellow sheets with my scribblings. I purposely set down my jottings far apart, leaving a generous amount of blank space in between them. This allows me to insert further notes in the spaces as I go along. For example, perhaps I've projected a tentative structure for Chapters 5 and 6. Then a new thought comes to me: I realize there is a block of material that could logically go in between those two chapters. On my notepad, this now becomes Chapter 5.1. Still another piece of subject matter may come drifting around after that, and this new piece may become Chapter 5.2. Eventually, of course, I will renumber everything in the conventional way.

Some writers use file cards for this preliminary organizing task. Others use cardboard accordion files with numbered pockets, each one representing a chapter, and they drop notes into the appropriate pockets as the outline-building process goes on. Every writer has his own system. One successful nonfiction writer I know jots his preliminary notes in a loose-leaf address book, the kind with tabs lettered from A to Z, each letter representing a chapter. He has been doing this for some twenty years. He is the only man I know who can tell you instantly, from memory, that J is the 10th letter of the alphabet and N the 14th.

You will undoubtedly develop your own system. The only advice I want to give you about it is that, whatever the system is, it should be set up so that the outline can begin constructing itself while you are writing your first chapter or two.

You are now well into the third step of building your samples-and-outline package. You find yourself sitting at your desk with a ragged sheaf of notepaper, or a bundle of thumb-smudged file cards, or a dented accordion file or something else that contains the unassembled bones of your book. The third and final step is to assemble them into a good, strong, logically designed skeletal structure.

In practice, probably some two-thirds of the outlines submitted to book publishers are arranged in chapter-by-chapter form. The writer has studied his projected subject material, has seen that it divides itself logically into fifteen or twenty segments, and has called each segment a chapter. In his outline, he numbers all the chapters and may also give them tentative titles.

Other writers' outlines are not formally segmented into chapters. Writers of such outlines believe they cannot predict the future course of their unwritten book clearly enough to organize it by chapters at this stage. Instead, their outlines merely attempt to describe the main areas of subject matter to be covered and the angles of attack by which these areas will be approached. Such outlines may have no numerical subdivisions or other formal structuring elements at all; in fact, they may not be much different from a long descriptive, well-organized letter.

It does not really matter what form an outline takes. What does matter, what is supremely important, is what the outline says.

It must be assumed at this point that your basic idea is a sound one. If it were not, your initial query would have drawn no enthusiastic response, and the publisher would not have invited you to submit an outline. Your outline should obviously reinforce the editor's original judgment about the soundness of the idea — should repeat all the selling points you made in your initial query. But the outline must do more than merely repeat: it must be the final convincer. Reading your query letter, the editor said to himself, "Well, yes, it sounds promising." Now you must make him say, "Yes! It's a book!"

There are three key points to bear in mind:

1. As a rule of thumb, your outline (not including the sample chapters that go with it) should probably be somewhere between three and eight single-spaced typewritten pages — or between six and sixteen double-spaced pages, if

you prefer. (The sample chapters should be double-spaced, since an editor may want to edit them later. He won't have any reason to edit your outline, so the spacing is up to you.)

Book editors don't usually like one- or two-page outlines. Not enough information is conveyed in an outline that short. The impression given is that the writer dashed it off in a hurry, without doing enough thinking about his project. On the other hand, editors are busy, and they are thankful for brevity. Twenty single-spaced pages would be too long an outline. An editor would be unhappy at the prospect of reading it, and it might also make him suspect that your book, should he encourage you to write it, will be too wordy.

2. Your sample chapters and outline, taken together, must strongly convey the impression that the book hangs together *as a single unit*. Don't let it deteriorate into a mere grab bag of random facts and fancies, loosely held together only by some vague relevance to your subject. Don't let the outline suggest that you have simply ambled around like a shopper at a supermarket, picking up a piece of subject material here and a piece there. Your book's main theme or themes, and its tone and emotional approach, must be apparent even in the necessarily terse wording of the outline.

To go to my *Very Rich* book as an example, I was worried right at the beginning that my outline would resemble a grab bag. The book was to be composed mainly of biographies of rich men. If my outline were simply a list of fifteen or twenty rich men, along with some random facts about them hastily garnered from an encyclopedia, it would not hold together as a single unit. To make it do so, I had to develop some strong thematic glue.

The glue was in the last half of the proposed title: . . . *and How They Got That Way*. My outline promised that every biography in the book would tackle its man from this special angle. *How* he got rich would be the overriding theme. The man's love life, his hobbies, his politics — neither these nor any other elements of a standard biography would share emphasis with that main theme. Such other elements might be mentioned in passing, to provide a splash of color, but in general they would not be pulled to stage center except where they cast light on the main question of how a man grew wealthy. I not only said this a number of times in my outline; I fear I harped on it more than was probably necessary. Still, it served its purpose. This thematic glue held the outline together — and, later, held the book together.

3. Your outline should provide a fair amount of detail on your proposed research sources.

In your first contact with the editor — your initial query letter — you persuaded him that you had a basically good book idea and that it was worth his while to listen to you further. Among other things, you made the book sound possible. You showed in a general way that the needed factual materials were available and that you could get to them. Now you must drive this point home. There is probably still a large and troublesome doubt lingering in the editor's mind, especially if you are a first-timer. While your sample chapters are convincing him that you have the required language mastery, your outline must convince him finally that the book is possible from the viewpoint of research.

Leave no further doubts in his mind. Tell him in detail that you know where and how you are going to do your research. Show him that there is enough of this factual material lying around to keep the book from becoming "thin" — too many words and not enough solid fact. And show him that you personally feel capable of going out and gathering this material.

V

PLANNING AND ORGANIZING

At the start of every nonfiction book project, the writer lives through a period of terror. It is inescapable. No matter how many books he writes, this period of panic returns with each new project.

For a first-book writer, and even for the veteran writer, this "terror" can cause a kind of paralysis of will. The paralysis is often called "writer's block" — as though to suggest that it is some special, romantic kind of malaise that attacks writers but nobody else.

I don't believe there is such a thing as "writer's block." Whenever you hear a writer moan that he is suffering from this mysterious sickness, you can come to one of two conclusions: Either he is just plain lazy, or he is troubled by the simple alarm that can attack anyone who is facing a large, complicated job. You can overcome this alarm or terror by the not very difficult act of organizing your book project in your mind.

Big projects lose their fearsomeness when organized. Broken down into units of work, divided into steps that can be taken one at a time, they always shrink to manageable size.

I remember well the panic that seized me when I set out to write my first book (*The Split-Level Trap,* published by Geis in 1960) in 1959. Frankly, I was scared. I lacked the comfort of knowing the book's future. There had been a grand feeling of success when the publisher accepted my outline and offered me a contract, but now that I faced the task of actually writing a 300-page book, the glow of optimism was gone. I had never before written anything longer than a three-part magazine article, amounting to perhaps 10,000 words. Now I was under contract to write 80,000 words in six months. The job looked nearly impossible.

I remember wandering around New York City for a couple of weeks, alternately pretending to do research and pretending I had writer's block. I was lying to myself on both counts. The truth was that I was simply avoiding the job ahead of me. It looked too huge.

One warm afternoon, I stepped out of the library to get some fresh air, ambled around the city for an hour and ended by sitting on a bench in a small park. Suddenly a lovely thought struck me.

The deadline for my book was six months away — six months, roughly 180 days. It abruptly came to me, as I sat gloomily on my bench, that I could easily finish the 300-page book in that time span by writing *only two pages a day*.

This was a pleasantly tranquilizing thought. It enabled me to see my book in small units of work, instead of looking aghast at the entire task. I buckled down to work on the following day, relaxed in the knowledge that I need write only two pages to count the day satisfactory. I was so relaxed that I wrote eleven pages. And so it went until the end of the project. I had the bulk of the book finished in three months.

Not all nonfiction writers organize book projects in this way. In fact, probably no two handle their work precisely the same, but all consistently successful ones employ some system of organization which effectively breaks the work into manageable stretches.

A nonfiction book generally implies two separate kinds of work: research and writing. The writer's problem is to synchronize these two tasks in a way that will produce a finished book by the deadline. There are two basic ways to approach this organizing and self-calming process.

The two-part approach: You research, then you write. If a writer has, say, six months to produce a book, he might assign the first three months to research and the last three months to writing. He would then further subdivide these units of time into smaller segments: three or four days for researching Chapter 1; two weeks or so for the longer and more difficult Chapter 2; and so on. He might do this in a strict and formal way, writing notes to himself on a calendar; or he might do it quite informally, keeping most of his self-imposed schedule in his head. Either way, however, he would arrive at a comforting vision of his project as a series of short steps.

The mixed approach: You research and write more or less simultaneously. You might start with a few days' research on Chapter 1. Then you spend a day or two writing the chapter. You get to page 6 and discover you need more facts. So you make a phone call, or you go out to spend an hour in the library. This research throws some new light on what you have already written, so you return to your typewriter and revise page 3. Then on to page 7 . . . and so on.

If this is your approach, your organizing method will necessarily be different from that of the writer who does all his research first. To block out your time from here to deadline day, you set minimum speed limits in terms of average pages per day or per week, or in terms of various chapters or sections that must be finished by certain dates.

I like the mixed approach myself. Neither approach is necessarily better than the other. Each writer must choose his own, and his choice will depend on his personality and his feelings about the task — and perhaps also on the type of book he is tackling. The mixed approach feels comfortable to me because I like frequent changes of activity and physical environment. I grow fretful when chained to my

typewriter for too many days in a row (which may be a reason why I'm not a novelist). Conversely, in the midst of research I often grow anxious to return to my typewriter and
get some complex thought on paper before it escapes. It is
a matter of intellectual style: the way my mind works. If
yours works differently, you should approach the organizing
task differently.

But whether you use the two-part or mixed approach, you
still face the need to block out your time. Organize it by
pages, by chapters, by chunks of subject matter, by other
manageable units, in a way that will make the whole job
end somewhere near — preferably before — the deadline.
And then hold yourself to the schedule.

Writers grumble a lot about deadlines, but in truth a deadline can be extremely useful — can be, in fact, the difference
between a book's coming into being or not. Novelists will
sometimes take five or more years to turn out a single book,
and maybe in novel writing that is all right. I strongly suspect
most of those super-long-term novels result either from
plain laziness or from the writer's need for self-dramatization.
(Fiction writers of my acquaintance seem to feel it is romantic to hang around in bars mumbling about writer's block.)
But most nonfiction books should be written faster. For one
thing, the factual content may be obsolete if you aren't quick.
For another thing, the close deadline forces you to battle your
own laziness and starting fears. Without a deadline you can
remain stalled and your book may never be written.

If a publisher has not given you a deadline, I strongly urge
you to impose one on yourself. If you plan to write full time,
six to nine months are usually ample for you to produce a
nonfiction book of average length and complexity. If you
can devote only part of your time to the book, two years
would be about the maximum you should allow yourself.
True, an occasional nonfiction project seems to require more

time than that. But as a general rule, if you find yourself taking more than nine months full time, or two years part time, you should ask yourself coolly and seriously whether you are simply trying to dodge the work.

As a matter of fact, a nonfiction book can be researched and written in six weeks if necessary. I do not counsel you to try this; I can tell you from experience that it is painful. But there is a point to be made about this, and it is a useful one for a beginner — for any writer — to bear in mind. Your capacity for work is much greater than you dream until you tap it. If you really *had* to write a book in six weeks, you probably could.

So don't let yourself be frightened by the work. In scheduling your project, set a reasonable pace for yourself. But make it a brisk pace, not an amble.

VI

FOR REFERENCE: PUBLIC AND PERSONAL LIBRARIES

Every time I write a book or a magazine article, I get stacks of letters from readers asking questions. Often the reader has gone to enormous trouble to find my address, or he has mailed his letter in care of the publisher and has waited weeks for the letter to be forwarded and for me to reply. (I always do reply, but often after a long delay and sometimes irritably.) And all the time, the answer to the reader's question lay waiting for him in his local library. He could have found his answer in five minutes.

I can only conclude that most people don't know how to use libraries. They seem unaware of the huge amount of information that can be stored even in a small town, either in the public library or in other collections of literature that are almost certain to be lying around here and there.

In the past ten years or so, I am happy to say, schools have paid more attention to this apparent gap in the public's education. Students are learning library research techniques along with math and English and biology. In some schools these library lessons are treated as minor and unimportant, but at least they are a step in the right direction. It could be argued that library lessons are the most important lessons of all. I value highly the facts and philosophies and opinions I learned about in school, but even more useful is the knowledge of *where to find out what I don't know.*

If you are a nonfiction book writer or aspire to be one,

you should thoroughly explore the library resources of your town. If you live in a small town or a suburb, as I do, you will also find yourself making occasional visits to the nearest big city or university library. But start in your own home town. You may be startled at the amount of data stashed within a mile or two of your front door. Of course, the more library work you can do near home, the fewer trips you will have to make to a city or college library — and the faster your book will get written.

Your obvious starting point will be the public library, if there is one, but don't stop there. Information valuable to a nonfiction writer is also likely to be tucked away in other book collections such as these:

Local school libraries. In my home town, for example, an excellent library in the junior high school contains several reference books that are not in the public library. The school can't have adults casually wandering in and out all day long, but by making arrangements with the librarian and by not abusing my privileges, I've been able to use that valuable library on occasion when I needed it.

Telephone-book library. Telephone books are among the most valuable reference works used by a nonfiction writer. Find out if a good phone-book collection exists near you. It is likely that your local phone company keeps such a collection, or perhaps the public library does. It should contain phone books of major cities around the nation, and these can save you hours of time.

Corporate libraries. If there are industrial companies or large office buildings near you, it is possible that one or more highly useful libraries are hidden in them somewhere. Many companies keep libraries — sometimes of a specialized nature, sometimes surprisingly broad-based (and sometimes including a phone-book collection).

Like schools, companies don't usually encourage the general public to use their libraries at will. But if you explain that you are a writer and need data for such-and-such a purpose, you will probably be given a cordial welcome. In more than twenty years of nonfiction writing, I have never asked a company for library privileges and been turned away.

State and town government libraries. There are likely to be mountainous stacks of data in state government bureaus near you, as well as at your local town clerk's office, tax collector's office, police station and elsewhere in and around the town or city hall. Often you can use these stored state and local facts to illustrate national trends and phenomena. If you are writing a book dealing with taxation, for instance, the data at your local town hall may actually be more revealing and compelling — because it is more intimate — than anything you are likely to find in Washington, D.C.

A warning: approach the town-hall folk with care and with a large smile. Government officials everywhere, from Washington to the smallest country town, tend to be nervous when dealing with the press. You may have to calm them down: convince them you do not intend to roast them in your book. Otherwise you may not win their fullest cooperation. They can't refuse to show you public documents, of course, but if they decide to be obstructive they can put all kinds of barriers in your way. It is better to have them as friends than as opponents.

After you get to know the libraries in your town, you will get to know certain time-saving books and will find yourself referring to these books over and over again. Below is a list of books that nonfiction writers probably consult most often. If you can't find them anywhere in your town, keep after the public librarian. Perhaps she can make room for them in next year's budget.

Book Review Digest. An annual publication that lists the more important books reviewed during the year and quotes briefly from the reviews. Every five years there is a cumulative index by subject matter. Consult these volumes whenever you are hit by a book idea; go back ten or fifteen years. This will tell you what other books have been written on your subject and what the critics did and did not like about them.

Readers' Guide to Periodical Literature. Lists, by subject matter, articles that have appeared in major magazines. Consult it to find what has been written on your subject in the past five or ten years. The articles will help you to build a background of fact and opinion, and will also lead you to sources of more information.

Specialized periodical indexes. The *Readers' Guide* does not list every periodical published in the country. If you are looking for material on a specialized subject, your librarian will be able to steer you to various other indexes that list publications in your field. Education, psychology, engineering: these and other specialties are covered by their own periodical indexes. In addition, most magazines index their own material and are generally happy to cooperate with writers trying to track the material down. *Playboy* and *True,* for example, are two major magazines that are not indexed in the *Readers' Guide,* for reasons that are obscure to me. If you are writing on a subject that you think these magazines may have covered in the past, simply write to them and ask for an index reading. (A letter addressed to "Editorial Librarian" will reach the right department.) Don't ask for copies of the magazines in which relevant material appeared. Ask only for a list of dates and page numbers, and then look up the back issues in a library.

New York Times Index. Lists, by subject, all the stories that have appeared in that weighty, often dull, always useful "newspaper of record." Even small libraries keep the Index, while the newspapers themselves are stored on microfilm in city and college libraries. (Your local librarian should know where.) Reading microfilmed newspapers is hard on the eyes — but it is still one of the quickest ways to gather data on topics of current interest.

World Almanac, New York Times Almanac and similar books. Annual publications. Current paperback issues can be bought for a couple of bucks at stationery stores; back issues can be found in most libraries. These books contain mountains of facts on thousands of topics. My personal collection goes back to 1947, and I don't believe I could ply my trade without it.

Telephone books. Outstandingly useful for tracking down sources. If your budget does not allow unlimited long-distance telephoning, you will have to do a lot of your research by mail. To do this successfully, you will need a quick way to find the addresses. Telephone books are the handiest of all reference volumes for this purpose.

The classified sections (yellow pages) are handy for a different purpose. They will help you gather lists of people or companies in a certain profession or business. If you are writing a book dealing with the theater, for example, the yellow pages will give you the names, addresses and phone numbers of theatrical agents, drama schools, set designers and dozens of other categories of people to whom you may want to go for information and opinion. No other reference source in the world contains so complete a listing of so many occupational categories.

Encyclopedias. Useful for historical fact, bibliographies and sources, but not generally useful for current facts. If you are writing a book about space exploration, for example, an encyclopedia will tell you what happened years ago, but the information will probably be sadly behind the times. Never use an encyclopedia as a sole source; always check current periodicals, newspapers and almanacs to bring yourself up to date.

Collected biographies. There are many compilations of short biographical sketches. Some are broad-based, like *Current Biography*. Others concentrate on people in a certain profession or a certain region, like *Who's Who in Commerce and Industry*. Use them to track down sources. A book may give you a man's complete address. Or it may tell you only what city he lives in or where he works, in which case a telephone book will lead you to the end of the trail.

U. S. Government publications. The Government publishes literally thousands of books and pamphlets on a huge variety of subjects. You can find a complete index of these publications in almost any medium-sized library. Many of the publications themselves will also be in the library — for instance, the annual *Statistical Abstract of the United States,* a thick and useful volume containing figures on everything from personal income to divorce rates to soybean crops. If a publication is not in your library, you can buy it from the Government Printing Office (Washington, D.C., 20402). Many of the pamphlets cost only 25¢ or so. If you wish, the Printing Office will send you, free, a monthly list of selected publications in subject areas of your choice.

As you pursue your writing career, you will probably want to build up your personal library. This need not be done right away, for you can always look up references in your local public library, but it can save you hours of time to buy your own inexpensive copies of certain books that you use frequently. Here are the ones that nearly every nonfiction writer keeps near his desk:

Dictionary. This may be the most expensive volume you buy. A small abridged dictionary is serviceable, but its usefulness to a writer is limited. I prefer a big dictionary, complete with synonyms, antonyms, comments on usage, a gazetteer and other handy elements. If you have a good enough dictionary, you probably won't need a thesaurus.

With luck and patience, you may be able to buy a big dictionary quite cheaply — or even get it free. It's a funny thing about dictionaries: they often tend to lie about, unwanted. People receive them as gifts and don't use them, or buy them for their kids, who go off to college. Once in a while, a public or corporate library will buy a new one and give the old one away. Dictionaries are always turning up at tag sales and church bazaars. If you keep your eyes and ears open, and let it be known around town that you want a full-sized dictionary, one may come your way fairly fast. I have two — a giant Random House and a two-volume Funk & Wagnalls — and I got both for nothing.

Almanac. Though you can find past issues of the *World Almanac* or *New York Times Almanac* at the local library, you may want to start buying the current issues from now on. The cost of the paperback editions ranges between two and four dollars, and in my opinion that money is worth spending. Almanacs are full of the kinds of factual material that can give a nonfiction book the sound of solid research, and you are likely to find yourself consulting your almanac several times a week.

There is only one thing that I find irritating about almanacs. They are always dated one year ahead, to make them sound more current than they really are. The almanacs dated 1973, for example, will actually contain the facts of 1972. If the year is 1973 and you want 1973 facts, you must go to some more current source such as the *New York Times Index.*

One-volume encyclopedia. Having a condensed encyclopedia near your desk can save you many trips to the library. You don't really need a complete, multi-volume set — although, if you can pick one up cheaply at a library sale, it will certainly do no harm. A one-volume encyclopedia can give you quick answers to the annoying questions that seem to come up again and again in nonfiction writing. When was the Battle of Waterloo? Who was Isocrates? It is highly irritating to be in the middle of a paragraph, discover that some obscure fact is missing, and spend an hour trudging to the public library and back when you really want to be home writing.

City phone book. You will find it extremely useful to keep on hand the phone book or books of the nearest big city. As I have said, alphabetical and classified phone books are valuable, each in its own way, for tracking down sources.

If you can show your local telephone company that you make frequent phone calls to the big city, the company may give you a set of city phone books for nothing. Otherwise, the charge will be a dollar or two.

Bartlett's Familiar Quotations. A handy volume, available in a cheap paperback edition. You will find it useful if in your writing you make occasional use of quotations from the past — a pleasant little habit that can add life to dull material, though it shouldn't be overdone.

Specialized references. Your personal library may also include reference volumes dealing with the subject area in which you concentrate. If you are a travel writer, for example, you'll find it useful to keep a set of travel guides and a good atlas on your bookshelf. I write frequently on the stock market, so I buy an annual market encyclopedia. One helpful fact is that, for anybody who can convince the Internal Revenue Service he is seriously in the writing business, many purchases of books and magazines are tax-deductible.

Only a minority of nonfiction books are built entirely from library research. Most depend more heavily on "live" sources — which is as it should be. If all books were written entirely with second-hand material drawn from other books and periodicals, we would be trapped in a closed circle of information, and eventually there would be no further reason to publish anything. It would all have been said before.

Except in the case of certain historical books, certain textbooks and a few other kinds, editors are pessimistic about any book whose author seems not to have stirred from the library. One requirement of a good book idea is that it sound new, and if your book is entirely or predominantly library-researched, this requirement will be hard to fulfill. As a general rule, you should use the library mainly for general background and for tracking down live sources. Avoid the temptation — common to beginners and old pros alike — to fill your book with easy-to-get, second-hand material.

Whenever you do use library material, be sure to give credit where it is due. This can be done informally, or it can be done by means of footnotes or a formal bibliography at the back of your book. I vastly prefer the informal method because it is more direct. It plants the credit right in the text of your book where every reader will see it, rather than in a list of notes or a bibliography that most readers will ignore.

In an informal credit, you need only identify the author and the book or periodical in which his work appeared. For example: "George Jones, writing in the *XYZ Review,* revealed some years ago that . . ." Or: "George Jones, in his autobiography, *Hey George,* tells the story of . . ." Those are informal credits. You work them right into your text as you go along.

Formal credits make more work for you — and at the same time are far less likely to be read. They are governed by certain stylistic conventions. For example, if you were writing a book in which you wanted to give formal credit to this one, your footnote or bibliography would contain this notation:

Gunther, Max. *Writing and Selling a Nonfiction Book.* Boston: The Writer, Inc., 1973.

Notice the order in which all those tidbits of data appear: the author's name, then the title, then the city of publication, then the publisher, then the year of publication. It all sounds very stilted, but this is how convention says it must be done.

Whether you use a formal or informal approach, be scrupulously careful to credit everybody whose work you use.

There is just one large class of data for which you do not need to give credit. "Common" facts and "common" news stories are generally considered to be in the public domain; they belong to anybody who wants to use them. A common fact is the kind of fact you can find in any encyclopedia or almanac: the political status of Spain in 1900, the date of Benjamin Franklin's birth, the population of California last year. Nobody owns these facts. In using them, you aren't required to say, "According to the Encyclopedia Americana . . ."

Similarly, news stories that have been widely reported are not considered to belong to any single newspaper or television newscaster. You aren't required to say, "According to the *Chicago Tribune,* President Nixon visited China in February, 1972."

But be careful. If the *Chicago Tribune* has run a special series of stories on local nursing-home conditions, or has assigned a reporter to interview a Presidential candidate in depth, these are not common news stories. They appear in one newspaper only. They belong to that newspaper. If you want to draw material from these stories, you must give credit.

It is usually quite easy to judge whether a fact or news story falls into this category of "common." If you are ever in doubt, give credit. It is far better to err in the direction of over-crediting than under-crediting.

VII

Getting Facts by Mail

When I started my writing career, it cost 3¢ to mail a first-class letter in the United States. Today it costs 8¢. I will not be surprised to see the price rise to 15¢ or even higher within this decade.

No matter. It will still be a bargain.

The U.S. Post Office, in fact, offers the world's best buy in communications. To a nonfiction book writer — and particularly to one who writes part-time and lacks time and money for long-distance traveling — the mail is an absolutely indispensable tool. Very rarely in this world is anything so valuable sold so cheaply.

By using the mail skillfully you can gather facts, opinions, quotes and other first-hand material nearly as effectively as you could through face-to-face interviewing. Did I say nearly as effectively? More so, sometimes. I remember working on a project years ago in which I wanted to get a statement of opinion from a well-known industrialist. I tried phoning him at his office a few times but his secretary barred the way like a sharp-fanged watchdog. She kept saying he was "in a meeting" and would call me back — but he never did. Other reporters told me the man had always been inaccessible to the press, and it was their opinion that I might as well give up. The man simply didn't like talking to journalists. His secretary had never been known to let one through.

So I looked up his home address (*Who's Who* gave me the

town; a phone book gave me the rest) and sent him a letter. He sent me a brief, pithy reply — precisely the kind of opinion statement I wanted.

In the normal course of events, a nonfiction book project begins with library research. You read what others have written on your subject in books, magazines, newspapers. This is all second-hand material. It is useful as general background, but in most cases it will not serve by itself as the building material for a new book. Sooner or later there must come a time when you stand up, leave that cozy library, go out into the world and track down some first-hand material. You do this either by in-person interviewing or by mail.

Your library research will have suggested sources of fact and opinion to whom you can write. As a matter of fact, the library research will often seem to give you everything you need to know on a certain subject. If you are writing a book about marriage and divorce, for example, a few hours of library digging will yield a long list of female liberationists who have strong opinions on the subject. You will walk out of the library knowing that a certain Miss Jones prefers to be addressed as Ms. and that she thinks marriage is an obsolete institution. You will be tempted to do no more digging and simply to report this second-hand fact in your book. *Resist the temptation.* A book made of second-hand material will not interest anybody — certainly not any editor worth his pay. Instead of taking this lazy route and dully repeating what others have written about Ms. Jones or what she has written about herself, find her address and write her a letter. Ask her to state her opinions to you directly. Word your letter in such a way that she will be likely to give you something fresh and new — something she hasn't said before, or hasn't said in quite that way.

To see this process at work, consider a research problem I tackled several years ago while writing a book called *The*

Weekenders. The book was a social-psychological study of how Americans use their weekends and why. My library digging yielded the name of one Dr. Alexander Reid Martin, a psychiatrist who had studied people's uses of leisure time. He appeared particularly fascinated by the type of man or woman who, instead of relaxing over the weekend, goes on working as though afraid to face what Dr. Martin called "unstructured time."

Dr. Martin's studies and opinions were obviously worth including in my book. I read several scholarly papers he had written and came out of the library with the feeling that I understood his views and findings pretty thoroughly.

I tried to write the chapter in which this material was to be included, and it came out as flat and cold as yesterday's pancakes.

I knew why. The problem was sheer laziness on my part. To avoid work, I was trying to build the chapter with second-hand material. The chapter was weighted down with too many heavy phrases like, "Dr. Martin wrote in 1962 that . . ." and "As Dr. Martin reported in the *Psychiatric Quarterly* in 1961 . . ."

The chapter had no chance to come alive that way. So I went back to the library and tracked down a mailing address for Dr. Martin. One of the scholarly journals for which he had written identified him as a member of the American Psychiatric Association, and the *World Almanac* gave me that association's address. I wrote to Dr. Martin. I asked him, in effect, to condense his views and findings into a few short paragraphs and tell them directly to me in a letter.

He sent me a friendly, detailed reply — exactly the kind of material I wanted. Now I was able to rewrite my drooping chapter by quoting the man directly: "Our culture is built on the ethic of work," says Dr. Martin . . .

The chapter came to life. Instead of leading my reader on a tour through a dusty library, I was letting him hear Dr.

Martin talk. Instead of telling him about material that had been written years before, I was telling him something he could take to be new.

How do you write letters that will bring the kinds of replies you want? There are nine rules that seem important to me:

1. Start by identifying yourself fully: "I'm a writer, and I'm working on a book about such-and-such." If you know who your publisher is going to be, name the company.

This self-identification is common courtesy. It is also very practical, for nobody is likely to reply to a question without knowing who the questioner is. If you simply wrote, "Dear Sir, Please tell me what your company has been doing about equal career opportunities for women," and if you failed to say who you were or why you wanted the information, your chances of receiving a reply would be slim.

2. Explain briefly (a sentence or two will usually do the trick) why you want the data or the statement of views you are requesting, and say how you plan to use this material in your book. You must remember that you are a total stranger to this man or woman whom you have buttonholed by mail. It is part of our human nature that, when a stranger asks us a question, we want to know why. If a stranger buttonholes you on the street and asks the time, you answer him because you can make assumptions about the reasons for his question. But if a stranger came up to you and asked, "Why are you wearing a blue coat?" your natural reaction would be another question: "Why do you ask?"

I usually fulfill this second rule by using some such phraseology as this: "One chapter of my book will deal with people who choose to go on working throughout the weekend, and I'd like to include the views and findings of professional observers such as yourself . . ."

3. Unless the answer is perfectly obvious, tell your source where you got his name and why you've singled him out to receive your letter. "I saw your name mentioned in an article in *XYZ Magazine,* and it occurred to me that you might be able to comment on this subject from the special viewpoint of . . ." Remember again that you are a stranger. In a minor sense, you are invading this man's or woman's privacy. There is probably some mystification in your source's mind; he wonders why you have abruptly dropped into his life from nowhere. You must put him at ease before he will unbend and answer your questions.

4. Use friendly, informal language. It is important to make the source *like* you, and you can't do this if your letter is cold and stiff, like a letter from a lawyer or a 19th-century businessman. But avoid using slang. For every ten people who don't object to slang, there is one who hates it violently — and this one may be your key source. A slangy letter may turn him off instantly. It may give him the impression that you are casual to the point of carelessness, and this may make him fear that you will use his data or opinions carelessly in your book, possibly doing him some damage in the process.

The impression you want to give is that you are a warm, amiable soul — but a careful and honorable one, too. Talk to your source as though you were sitting across a dinner table from him. Your purposes can't be served either by sitting stiffly at attention (lawyer language or commercialese) or by slouching and spilling gravy down your front (slang) .

5. Ask *only* simple, specific questions — only the kinds of questions that can be satisfied with short replies. *Do not* ask your source to write a ten-page essay in reply. He won't. You are asking him to do too much work for you. In fact, he probably won't reply at all.

This is one of the most difficult rules to fulfill. Often, you will find yourself in the position of wanting exactly what you cannot ask for: an essay. The subject may be a complex one, and you want your source to give you all his thoughts on it. What can you do? There are two ways out of the dilemma. You can ask the source to grant you an in-person or telephone interview (see Chapter VIII), or you can word your letter in such a way that he will be tempted to write you an essay even though you have not asked for one.

This is not as hard to do as it may seem. If you have picked your source carefully, the likelihood is that he knows a lot about this subject on which you have approached him, considers himself to be an expert in it, has some strong feelings about it, is anxious to have the facts as he sees them laid down properly. If you ask him only two or three short, specific questions, he may feel his answers to those questions won't explain his views fully enough. He may end by writing you the essay that you were too courteous to ask for.

This happened to me in 1968, for instance, when I was working on a book called *Casebook of a Crime Psychiatrist.* It dealt with the adventures of Dr. James Brussel, who used his knowledge of the criminal mentality to help the New York police track down a number of famous criminals. One such criminal was the so-called "Mad Bomber," who terrorized New York for more than a decade by placing bombs in public buildings. Seeking detailed data on the Mad Bomber, I wrote a letter to a now-retired New York police official who (according to several newspaper accounts) had been involved in the years-long investigation.

It was a difficult letter to write. What I really wanted to ask the man was, "Tell me everything you remember about the Mad Bomber. . . . Write me a 50-page memoir. . . ." Obviously, such a request would simply have stunned the man with its enormity. He probably would have dropped my letter into a wastebasket, considering it unanswerable.

Instead, I carefully composed five short questions, each of

which could be answered with a simple "Yes" or "No." I asked, for instance, "Was there ever a time, during this decade, when the investigation was abandoned as hopeless?" And: "It was reported several times in the papers that you believed there might be more than one Mad Bomber. Is this true?" And so on.

These were leading questions, needling questions. If the man so chose, he could have sent me the following reply: "Dear Mr. Gunther: No, Yes, Yes, No, Yes." But if I knew anything at all about human nature, I thought, it would be nearly impossible for him to do that. He would hardly be able to resist embellishing his yeses and noes. The subject was too complex to be satisfied with such simple replies. As I mailed the letter, I felt quite confident that he would answer each question with at least a short paragraph of explanation — and that, if I was lucky, he would in fact write me an essay.

That is precisely what he did. His reply covered six single-spaced pages.

6. Address every information-please letter to an individual man or woman, never to an organization.

If you are writing a book in which you need data about automobile exhausts and air pollution, for example, one obvious source would be General Motors Corporation. But if you address your letter simply to GM, your chances of getting a useful reply are not good. Your letter will simply drift around that huge organization and quite possibly, after a while, disappear. Each man or woman on whose desk it lands will pass it along to somebody else. Nobody will want to take on the irksome responsibility of replying. If you are lucky, your letter may finally amble its way to the desk of someone who will make a conscientious effort to reply — but only if you are lucky.

You vastly improve your chances by addressing the letter

to a specific individual. Any time you are seeking data or opinion from an organization in which you know nobody by name, ask yourself two questions: whose responsibility will it be to reply, and who will *want* to reply? Usually both questions will point to a single individual. In the rare cases where two people seem indicated, write to both.

In nearly all industrial companies and most large non-profit institutions — hospitals, foundations, associations — the man or woman to write to will be the Public Relations Director. (Sometimes his title is Publicity, Press, Press Relations or News Director, or something else; but if you address him as Public Relations Director, your letter will get to him.) In most federal, state and big-city government bureaus, the person holding this job is called the Director of Public Information. Whatever the title is, the job is to deal with the press; and if you're a nonfiction book writer, that's you. The publicity or information chief is paid to get his organization favorably mentioned and its views explained in magazines, newspapers, TV broadcasts and books. If he does not know the answers to your specific questions, he will make it his business to put you in touch with somebody in the organization who does.

If you are seeking information from a smaller organization — a suburban real estate company, for example, or a small-town tax assessor's office — the staff is not likely to be big enough to include a public relations or information chief. In this case, send your letter to the chief executive. Address it to "The President," or "The Tax Assessor." If the top man doesn't want to reply to your letter, he will probably instruct one of his subordinates to reply.

If the company is located in your city or nearby, you will be able to get the name of the president, public relations director, chief engineer, or whomever you wish, simply by telephoning and asking the operator (or Information, if the firm is large enough) for it. In this way you can address him or her by name in your letter, usually increasing your chance of getting the information you want promptly.

7. Always imply that you are up against a close deadline, even though you are not. Ask your source to reply as soon as he can. Some people have the pleasant habit of answering their mail promptly, but many do not — and this includes many overworked people in large organizations. Unless you say you need the reply quickly, your source may slip your letter into his "tomorrow" file along with a bundle of overdue bills and charity solicitations. You may not hear from him for weeks, or ever.

Remember to use friendly, informal language. Don't use any of those stiff and ugly phrases from the lexicon of commercialese: "Trusting this matter will receive your prompt attention, I remain . . ." Instead, tell the man what you want in plain English: "My deadline is creeping up on me, so I'll be grateful if you can answer my questions as soon as it's convenient . . ." Or, if you are really up against it, give *him* a deadline: "My deadline is uncomfortably close. Do you suppose you can give me some answers by next Tuesday, April 15?"

As long as you have carefully observed the rule that forbids you to ask for an essay in reply, the chances are good that your source will honor your request for promptness. He may even send you the essay you haven't asked for. One man even sent me an audio tape cassette. His recorded voice began: "I wanted to get this to you in time for your deadline, and since I don't have time to write it, I'm recording it in my car on the way home from work. Your questions raise a lot of complicated points . . ."

8. If your subject is an emotional or controversial one, or if you suspect for any other reason that your source will be nervous about replying, offer to let him read and pencil-edit

what you write before publication. You must put him at ease.

It is a nuisance, of course, to submit parts of manuscripts to sources in this way. It can drive you half crazy. The more you can avoid the nuisance, the more peaceful your life will be as you near the end of your book project. Don't make such pre-editing offers promiscuously. And when you do feel it is necessary to make such an offer, word it in such a way that the source must ask for it before you actually send him anything.

In other words, don't make a flat promise in your initial information-please letter that you are going to mail a piece of manuscript to the man. Instead, say that you will do this if he wants you to — but make him say so first. I usually word the offer something like this: "I'll be happy to show you the sections in which you're quoted, if you think it will be helpful." This isn't a flat promise. Before I am morally obliged to do anything about it, the source must write back and say, "Yes, show me the sections." My hope, obviously, is that he won't. As long as I've been careful with the language and tone of my letter — as long as I come out sounding like a careful and honorable reporter — the chances are good that the source will not, in fact, take me up on my half-hearted offer.

9. Always write back and thank any source for his or her reply. You never know when you might want to call on this man or woman again.

This ninth rule is particularly important if you plan to specialize, or sense that you might end by specializing, in a certain area of subject matter. I am not actually a specializing writer, but in my twenty-plus years in the business I've found myself returning again and again to two subject areas: the occult and the stock market. Many of my best sources in both these areas are people I have never met face-to-face, nor even talked to by phone. They are people with whom I exchange letters. Each time I tackle a new project in one or the other of these two areas, I start by writing information-please letters to this helpful little band of pen pals.

When I took on a book project that straddled both subject areas at once — the book was *Wall Street and Witchcraft,* a study of occult and mystical approaches to the stock market — I calculate that I got at least half of the book's meat and bones by mail.

VIII

INTERVIEWING

A. J. Liebling, one of the cleverest interpretive reporters ever to be turned loose on the national scene, once made some remarks in *The New Yorker* that should be of great comfort to a beginning nonfiction book writer. "There is almost no circumstance under which an American doesn't like to be interviewed," Liebling wrote. "We are an articulate people, pleased by attention, covetous of being singled out."

Indeed we are. If you are starting a nonfiction career and are worried about your ability to be a good reporter, your capacity to draw facts and opinions out of people, take Liebling's words to heart.

What he said, in effect, was that there is no reason to be frightened at the prospect of interviewing somebody, for the very strong likelihood is that the man or woman *wants* to be interviewed.

Beginning nonfiction writers do tend to approach this part of the game with a certain degree of fright. If you have never interviewed anybody before, you probably harbor such fears of your own. This is perfectly natural: nearly any new experience looks scary when we first tiptoe up to it. But take it from Liebling and take it from me: once you have completed your first plunge, you will discover interviewing is really the easiest and in many ways the most enjoyable aspect of the whole nonfiction writing business.

When you go to interview somebody, either by phone or in person, don't ever go with the negative feeling that this man or woman will consider you a nuisance, that you are imposing, that you are invading privacy. Once in a while you will meet a withdrawn and prickly person with that kind of reaction, but only once in a while. In nearly every case the interviewee will be delighted to talk to you — would be quite disappointed, in fact, if you were to call the interview off.

Some interviews obviously go better than others. Even Liebling had his failures. But you can count on a fair share of good interviews if you follow the six rules below. As you gain more experience you will undoubtedly refine your interviewing technique and increase your share of successes still more.

1. Except in the rare case where you must act very fast, always phone or write for an appointment a week or more before you want the interview to take place. Do this even though you plan to conduct the interview by phone. Ask your proposed source to set a date and hour when he can talk to you conveniently, and then phone him back (or visit him, as the case may be) at that exact hour.

There are two good reasons for doing this. One has to do with common courtesy. Wrongly used, a telephone can be an instrument of extreme rudeness. It is not a good idea, when avoidable, to drop into somebody's life by phone and abruptly ask him to give you half an hour or more of his time right then and there. Daily newspaper reporters often have to do this, but as a book writer you lack the excuse of daily deadlines. The source can reasonably assume the interview will be as useful to you next week as this week, and if you ask him to do it right away he may be irritated.

The second good reason for this non-abrupt interview technique is that, by making an appointment a week or more in the future, you give the source time to collect his or her thoughts on your subject. I recently began work on a book for Doubleday, dealing with an aspect of city office buildings. One old building in New York intrigued me for a number of reasons, and I phoned the building's rental agent to see what he knew about its history. He seemed to know a good deal and was willing, even eager, to talk to me right then and there on the phone. But I said I would rather drop around and talk to him in person the following week. We set an hour and date. By the time I showed up for the interview, he had collected a pile of documents and fascinating trivia bearing on the old building's history. "The old place is even more interesting than I thought," he said. I went away from the interview with a notebook full of unusual and compelling material -— very little of which would have come to light if I hadn't given my source a week to mull over the subject.

2. When writing or phoning for an interview appointment, identify yourself and your book as fully as possible, and tell the source precisely where he or she fits in. I usually open the initial phone call with some such phraseology as this: "Mr. Jones? My name is Max Gunther. I'm a writer, and I'm working on a book about such-and-such. Since you're in the this-and-that business, I thought maybe you could give me a little information."

At this point, Jones usually mumbles something like, "Sure I'll give you what help I can . . ." But he sounds somewhat puzzled. I'm a total stranger who has suddenly turned up from nowhere. Jones has many questions in his mind. Why have I picked *him* instead of some other source? Where did I get his name? And what *is* this book I've mentioned? Why am I writing it? From what angle will I approach the subject?

My job now is to put all these mysteries to rest in Jones' mind, so that he sees exactly where he stands in relation to me and my project. I tell him everything I think he might want to know. The object is to make me something other than a total stranger. I tell him who will publish the book, if I know that fact — or who I hope will publish it, if I am in a preliminary outline-writing or selling phase of the project. I tell him about other people in his trade or profession whom I've interviewed or plan to interview. I explain why I've singled him out. I say precisely why I think he will be helpful and precisely what aspects of the book's subject I want him to talk about. By the time I finish, if I have done it right, Jones is relaxed. I am no longer a stranger. I'm an amiable fellow asking a perfectly reasonable favor — the granting of which, from Jones' point of view, promises to be fun.

As soon as I hear the puzzlement vanish from Jones' voice, I ask him to set an hour and date for the interview.

3. Do everything possible to make the interview leisurely. Your source may have some time pressures on him, but make sure there are none on you. Don't make other appointments close to the interview hour if you can avoid it; let your source ramble on as long as he wants to. Don't *ever* begin an interview by deadlining it: "I've only got until 3:30, so I hope we can cover everything in an hour . . ."

If I sense a man or woman will be unusually helpful and talkative, I try to allow much more than an hour of time. In the case of a phone interview, I ask the source to talk to me in the evening, from his home, rather than from his office during working hours. People are generally more relaxed in the evening; their time is not so inflexibly scheduled as during the average day. I never tell the source in advance that I think the interview may last two hours, for that might frighten him. I simply make room for a long, leisurely interview in case it turns out that way. Similarly, in the case of face-to-face interviews, I like to make appointments for 11 a.m. or 4 p.m. This way, if we go beyond an hour and I want the source to go on talking, I can take him out for lunch or a drink.

4. Let the source do all the talking he wants to do, and let him do it in his own way. The least productive interviews are those in which the reporter keeps jumping in with questions, as though he were a lawyer cross-examining a witness. As A. J. Liebling once put it, "If you make a man stop to explain everything he will soon quit on you, like a horse that you alternately spur and curb."

Unless you are writing an exceptionally dry kind of book, you need more than dry facts to fill it, to bring it alive. Your purpose in conducting an interview is partly to get facts, yes — but you also want color; you want anecdotes; you want quotes; you want material that will give readers an impression of the interviewee's personality. You can hardly hope to gather such material if you structure the interview rigidly. Contrary to what you'll see in the movies, a good reporter very seldom spends a whole interview peppering a source with questions. Instead, a good reporter asks a few questions in the beginning, to get things started. Then he sits back and lets the source tell the story in his own way, at his own pace.

Before showing up for an interview, I try to think of "starter" questions that will get the source going on the subject I want to hear about. If all goes well, the starter questions wind him up like a clock, and I quietly fall back from the status of questioner to that of listener. If he omits some area of subject matter that I want to hear about, or if he explains something inadequately, I resist the temptation to interrupt him. I wait until he winds down, then wind him up again by asking the questions he has left unanswered.

5. Make all your questions specific, sharply focused on small areas of your subject. Large, vague, general questions are unanswerable.

As an example, I went to New York one wintry morning in 1972 to interview a former agent of the Internal Revenue Service. Another IRS agent had submitted his memoirs to Playboy Press, and these memoirs, though compelling, were thin, unfocused, and badly organized. My assignment was to flesh out the material and rewrite the memoirs to produce a salable book. To do this, I had to talk to a long list of tax experts and IRS folks, hoping to gather anecdotal and other material that the author-agent and I could weave into the book.

When I walked into that interview with the ex-agent in New York, I had no really clear idea of what I wanted him to tell me. Basically, I wanted him to ramble. I wanted him to tell me everything interesting that had ever happened to him in his tax-collecting job. But how could I get him started?

I could have asked a vague, general question: "Has anything exciting ever happened to you in your IRS job?" I *could* have asked that, but I didn't. The question was too broad. It would simply have buffaloed the man.

Instead, I focused down sharply on a small area of this huge subject. My starter question was, "When you were auditing people's tax returns, did anybody ever try to bribe you?"

That question wound him up — in fact, very nearly overwound him. I saw I had touched a nerve. He talked emotionally about that subject for a while, and then that subject suggested others, and those suggested still more. He talked for four hours, right through lunch. I barely asked another question the whole time, and I came out of the interview with a wealth of fascinating material about the inner workings of IRS. My great, broad question — "Did anything exciting ever happen. . .?" — had been fully answered without ever being asked.

6. Be sure your reportorial paraphernalia never gets in

the way and interrupts the source's flow of thoughts. If you must use a tape recorder, at least use a small, inobtrusive one whose microphone need not be held up before the source's face. If you use a notebook, use a small looseleaf or spiral-bound one whose pages can be turned without making a loud crackling noise. And never, *never* ask the source to stop or slow down so you can catch up with your note-taking. If you fall behind, the reason probably is that you are trying to take down the source's words too fully. Only a tenth of the average talker's total word output is really meaningful. With experience you will learn to recognize what is meat and what is mere fat. And, as all reporters do, you will develop your crazy style of shorthand, intelligible only to you. Nobody ever talks fast enough or meatily enough to get ahead of a practiced reporter.

I seldom use a tape recorder because such gadgetry turns some people off, particularly in interviews dealing with emotional or controversial subjects. Often I don't even use a notebook. Some kinds of people are rendered nervous by any kind of note-taking. They talk more fluently when the reporter simply slouches in a chair or stands around with his hands in his pockets, as in a casual conversation between friends. You will discover, after walking out of an interview with no notes, that you can recall everything of real importance that was said.

IX

THREE ELEMENTS OF STYLE

Every good nonfiction writing style has three major attributes: clarity, force and color. Let's see what these attributes are and how you achieve them.

Clarity is the most self-explanatory of the three terms. A clear style is one that puts its meanings across to the reader easily and quickly and straightforwardly, one that does not require him to puzzle, wonder, reread. To achieve clarity, you have to look hard at every sentence and paragraph you write, and ask yourself whether its meaning will be as clear to other people as it is to you.

This is a difficult trick, one that some otherwise literate people never seem to master. But a writer must master it. You stand back from your work and ask, what does it really *say?* Even after writing professionally for more than twenty years, I am still very often chagrined to find that what I *thought* I was saying is not in fact what my typewriter has said.

A lack of clarity can result from plain, careless ambiguity. For example, in my book, *The Weekenders,* one of my first-draft sentences went like this:

> A suburbanite may scorn a city-dweller because he doesn't know what creeping red fescue is.

That inept sentence was perfectly clear to me when I wrote

it, but when I read it over, I saw it would not be clear to anybody else. Who doesn't know what creeping red fescue is — the suburbanite or the city dweller? After considerable rearranging, I finally came out with a sentence that read:

A suburbanite does not do the same things on weekends as a city-dweller, who may believe that creeping red fescue is some kind of loathsome disease.

The common mistake of trying to pack too many thoughts together too densely can also cause lack of clarity. For example, consider this early-draft sentence from another of my books:

A man who, having bought some stock or made other investments early in his life, finds his financial circumstances changing to such an extent that he can't recall just why he found those investments attractive, may be well advised to sell out and buy something else.

That is a sentence of perfectly logical construction, and a reader coming to it fresh and bright-eyed would probably have no trouble digesting its meaning. But a tired reader, or one troubled by distractions, as in a noisy household, might get tangled up in the middle. There are too many thoughts between the opening phrase and the close. I chopped the sentence into more manageable fragments, like this:

A man may buy some stock or make other investments early in his life, but then his financial circumstances change. He finds himself wondering why those investments attracted him. In a case like this, he will usually feel happier and may feel richer (and might even become richer) if he sells out and buys something else.

(Note that, in the process of reworking this passage, I killed the hackneyed little phrase, "may be well advised to." This was a case of making the style my own.)

It is hard work to achieve perfect clarity. As a matter of fact ambiguity of a sentence, phrase, or even a word most often results from a writer's laziness. He may be trying to write too quickly; he may set down his thoughts in the jumbled order in which they pour from his head; he may not be willing to stand back from his work and ask whether his meanings will jump across to the reader quickly and lucidly.

It isn't that your reader is stupid or must be treated like a child. On the contrary, it is likely that he is smart enough to recognize bad writing very quickly when he sees it. There is an enormous amount of reading material competing for his attention in his limited spans of free reading time. Obviously, he will choose those books that give him the greatest rewards for the least effort. It would be very arrogant of you to suppose that your thoughts are more compelling than other writers', and that a reader will willingly struggle through dense, unclear language to find out what you mean to say. He won't. And most emphatically, an editor at a publishing house won't.

Force is the quality of saying things strongly. This does not mean you must shout at your reader all the time or end every other sentence with an exclamation mark. (In fact, frequent use of exclamation marks is a symptom of weak writing. Force comes from words themselves. If they are not forceful, no amount of artificial juicing-up with punctuation marks will be likely to help.) Some recent angry books on ecology and race relations have been written in a steady shout, but that is not usually necessary. Force in writing, as I define it, means saying things emphatically when emphasis is called for. It means ending each statement of a thought — each paragraph, each section, each chapter — with a good, solid, final thump.

A perfect example of weak writing appeared in the 1971 Federal Income Tax Forms. I appreciate that the U. S. Government may sometimes have good reasons for mumbling instead of speaking plainly, and that these considerations can lead unavoidably to weak writing. Still, the income tax package is among the most egregiously public of all public documents (some 100 million copies are printed and distributed each year: a best seller on a grand scale), and we are certainly at liberty to subject the package to literary criticism. So let's consider the "Special Message from the Commissioner" that was printed on the front of the 1971 package. The first paragraph read:

> We know that filling out a tax return is not fun — even if you get a refund, which most taxpayers do. Yet, we believe most American taxpayers can make their own tax return for 1971.

Aside from its jumpy punctuation and imprecise grammar (no comma is necessary after "Yet," and the word "return" in the same sentence ought to be plural), this gummy little paragraph has all its potential emphasis spread out and dissipated somewhere in the middle. It starts to say something, falters, then goes on to mumble about something else. It doesn't end with a solid thump; it merely meanders its way toward the final period. And because of its lack of force, its meaning is not really very clear. It seems to be saying, "Filling out tax returns isn't fun, but most people can do it." The connection between the two thoughts is not immediately apparent. Why need something be fun in order to be easy to do?

There are dozens of conceivable ways in which this paragraph could have been written more forcefully. Here is one:

> We know that filling out a tax return is not fun. But we believe most American taxpayers will at least find the task relatively easy. Most will be able to make out their own returns for 1971. And we would like to point out that, for most, the fun will come later. Most taxpayers get refunds.

Written that way, the paragraph ends with a small but distinct thump. The reader has been pulled into one end of the paragraph and pushed out the other. The degree of force is not great, but it is a force that the reader can feel. He knows the direction in which the author wants him to travel. He can feel himself being pushed — gently in this case, but insistently — in a straight line from the first sentence to the last.

Force in writing starts with deciding exactly what impact you want each paragraph to have on the reader. Once you know this, you arrange the paragraph's component thoughts in a way that will make emphasis come at the end and the whole paragraph drive straight toward that end. On a larger scale, the same kind of force should be felt driving through other components parts of your book: through the various sections within your chapters, through each chapter, and through the entire book. At the end: *thump.*

Never start a paragraph unless you know essentially how you want it to end. Never let a paragraph wander at random. If you find a paragraph going nowhere in particular, there is only one thing to do. Kill it and start again.

Color is the quality that makes writing attractive, interesting, fun to read. If an author writes colorfully, a reader may be drawn to the words even though he has no particular interest in the subject matter. He derives entertainment from the play of words themselves. Conversely, colorless writing can bore a reader to sleep even though he is acutely concerned with the subject matter. It is even possible to write colorlessly about such a vibrantly colorful subject as sex.

Color in language comes partly from structural variety. Vary the lengths of your paragraphs, the lengths and structures of your sentences. Some writers like to jolt the reader once in a while with a one-sentence paragraph or a one-word sentence, particularly in places where emphasis is called for.

Others derive refreshment from an occasional incomplete sentence. Like this.

Watch carefully for any tendency toward monotony in your writing. If you find you have strung together a long limp rope of straight declarative sentences with two commas in the middle, like this one, chop some of them into two or turn them inside-out or back-to-front. Monotony generally comes from laziness, from saying things in a mechanical way that comes easily. You have to be alert to the possibilities of language. Continually ask yourself, "Can I say it better? Is there a way that would be more colorful, more original, more satisfying?"

Take the simple little sentence, "Therefore, he went to New York." It is a perfectly good sentence, and there might be many stylistic situations in which it would serve well. But suppose there is a situation where monotony has set in. The sentence can be written in a lot of other ways:

So off to New York he went.

And where did he go? New York.

Destination: New York.

And so on. An alert writer would tinker with such possibilities, either on paper or in his head. He might end by discarding them all and returning to the original sentence. But he would at least ask himself whether more colorful language is possible. No good writer ever assumes that the first words to tumble from his typewriter are the best possible words.

Color comes not only from variety, but also from a careful selection of words and phrases that have their own intrinsic life, bounce and energy. This does not mean what some amateur writers appear to think it means: loading your language with great, gaudy festoons of adjectives, adverbs, ing-words and other qualifiers ("the huge, black, ponderous locomotive ground slowly and protestingly to a screeching, clanking, spark-spitting halt . . ."). It means, instead, picking words and building phrases and sentences that will provide flashes of color without slowing the momentum of your language. The color should seem to spring from *within* the language. If you simply string qualifiers together, the color seems to have been splashed on from outside, as an afterthought.

Let me give you an example from one of my books, *Wall Street and Witchcraft*. I don't consider this book to be a paragon of colorful writing. As a matter of fact, much of the language I used in it is plain to the point of drabness, for I was dealing with such strange subject matter (the use of occult arts in the stock market) that I felt obliged to tone my language down deliberately to a reportorial monotone in some passages. All the same, there were parts of the book in which I worked hard to introduce flashes of color.

At one point, I was describing a visit I made to New York's financial district — the Wall Street area — late one rainy night. I wanted to put my own emotions into the writing. I tried it like this:

> . . . The narrow, twisted streets, densely crowded all day, were dark, empty, eerily lonesome in the rain . . .

Somehow that sentence, when I read it over, reminded me of a high-school attempt at poetry. It was overloaded with adjectives and adverbs. Moreover, it had a hackneyed quality. It was full of standard ghost-story words: "dark . . . eerily . . . rain . . ." A reader would recognize this gluey bundle of words for what it was: a clumsy attempt to put him in the mood to hear stories of the occult.

Whenever you find you have applied color so clumsily that your intentions stand out, it's time to rewrite. I did. In my second attempt, I abandoned the approach of splashing on color dipped from a bucket of cliché ghost-story words. Instead, I simply described what I saw. Here is how the passage finally appeared in print:

The narrow, twisted streets, densely crowded all day, were nearly empty. In the coffee shops a few secretaries and late-working executives and night computer attendants sat and ate their lonesome suppers or breakfasts, gazing out morosely at the rain . . .

That created the mood I wanted to create. It did so without using artificial words, and without waving a flag that said, "Note! Color!"

X

MAKING THE STYLE YOUR OWN

Though all good writing styles share the three attributes of clarity, force, and color, it is obvious that not all styles are alike. In fact the individuality of a writer's style — the personal element that distinguishes it from other writers' styles — is one of the things that make it attractive.

This is a lesson that every beginner must learn. You can study other writers' work at great length to see how they handle the language, and you can listen to writer-teachers like me as we try to give you some preliminary guidance. But the job of developing a unique style is essentially a lonely job. The style you develop should not be mine or any other writer's. It should be yours.

A writer's style is ideally like his voice on the phone. It is distinctly his, immediately recognizable to those who are familiar with it. Yet it is also changeable, adaptable, flexible. Without losing its own distinctive qualities, it can be made to serve in an infinite variety of situations. It can express anger or pleasure, fear or joy — yet through all these modifications, it remains the same voice, as recognizable in one mood as in another.

The elements that personalize a writing style are not easy to pick out, any more than are those of a voice on the phone. The American Telephone & Telegraph Company tried to find out how people identify each other's phone voices — what elements of timbre, accent, word choice and rhythm help you recognize the voice of a friend or family member without his needing to announce who he is. The company concluded in the end that the process is too complex and subtle to be analyzed mechanically. And so it is with writing style. We could spend weeks picking out the stylistic differences among nonfiction book writers such as Winston Churchill, William L. Shirer and John Gunther, but no amount of analysis could totally explain each man's special stylistic impact. We would be reduced to saying, in the end, "Well, they just *sound* different."

As a beginner, you must develop a style that has this special, personal sound — the sound of *you*. The book ideas you submit to publishing companies will begin the necessary process of attracting editors' attention to your work, but ideas alone aren't enough. It is quite likely that any idea you submit will already have been thought of in different forms by other people — probably by other writers, perhaps by the very editor who reads your outline. The book represented by the idea hasn't yet been written, mainly because the right writer and the right form of the idea have not yet come together. Your writing style will tell the editor whether, in his opinion, you are or are not the right writer. If your style is pedestrian, imitative, uninteresting, the editor will say, "Well, no, if I want that book written at all, I'll get so-and-so to write it." Obviously that isn't what you want him to say. The reaction you want is, "Yes! *This* is the writer for this idea!"

How do you make your style yours? One odd little piece of advice that you occasionally hear bandied about in this business is, "Write as you speak." Well, perhaps. But that advice grossly oversimplifies a complicated question. If you followed the advice literally, you would never sell a word.

For one thing, spoken language is full of hesitations, repetitions, meaningless noises and other imprecisions that simply don't belong on paper. Even highly literate people sound foolish when their spoken words are transcribed literally to paper.

For another thing, spoken communication depends heavily on gestures, facial grimaces, voice inflections and other signals that can't be translated into print. The simple little phrase, "Oh, boy," for example, can be spoken so as to express dozens of possible meanings ranging from disgust to delight. On paper, the phrase is virtually meaningless unless the writer has very carefully established it in a certain context — and he must do this with words, not with voice tones or shrugs or grimaces.

So you can't really write as you speak. But the advice does have a core of truth in it, as long as you don't take it too literally. It becomes a more useful piece of advice, more meaningful, if we change it to read, *Write as you think.*

As *you* think. You personally.

This means that your words should always describe *your* feelings about a subject, not some other writer's feelings. It is an unfortunate fact that we writers — especially when we're trying to write in a hurry — tend to use other people's words and phrases because it's easier that way. Beginners and veterans alike fall into this bad habit. The only way to cure it is to stay eternally vigilant when rereading your own work. Eye it sourly. Whenever you come across a phrase that has a too-familiar ring, kill it. They aren't your words and they don't express your feelings. Ask yourself, "How do I really feel about this? What image does it conjure up for *me?*"

The most obvious examples of lazy writing are those worn-out phrases that we call clichés. "As alike as two peas in a pod . . . peaches-and-cream complexion . . . eating like a horse . . . trees stood like sentinels . . ." Soggy bundles of words like these do not belong in good writing. If you want to describe a girl's complexion, forget about peaches and cream. That is some other writer's image, not yours. Ask yourself how the girl's skin looks to you. What are your own images? Your own feelings?

Clichés are easy to recognize. The loud, dull clang of familiarity rings unmistakably in the ear, and even a beginner can learn to keep it out of his work in short order. But there is a vastly larger class of other phrases which, although they can't quite be called clichés, nonetheless are worn at the edges from too frequent use. It is almost impossible to write a page of manuscript without using phrases that others have used before, and you can't hope to weed every familiar phrase from your work. (Rereading this paragraph, I note with some disgust that I've used the familiar old phrase, "in short order." Normally I'd kill it on recognizing it, and I'd substitute my own words. I've left it in to show how easily such phrases can sneak into a writer's work when he isn't looking — can sneak in even when he is busily writing about the very subject of clichés.) But although you can hardly hope to delete all the familiar phrases, you can hope — and in fact should deliberately plan — to throw out large numbers of them. Whenever you can, use your own words or combinations of words.

This is how the development of personal style begins. Every professional writer could give you hundreds of examples of cases in which he threw out other people's phrases and substituted his own. It probably happens at least once per page. Sometimes the substitution takes place in the writer's head (that's when he is fresh and alert), and at other times it takes place on paper.

Glancing through my own book manuscripts, I see a huge variety of examples that I could give you. Let's just pick one at random.

Here is a phrase from the rough draft of my Playboy Press book on the Internal Revenue Service. I was talking about a sour old revenue agent, and in this draft I mentioned that he "took an immediate dislike to" a certain young taxpayer.

Later, I crossed that phrase out. The messiness of the manuscript at this point indicates that I tried several other ways of wording the thought. I finally ended by saying that the old agent "began by enthusiastically disliking" the taxpayer.

Why? Well, to begin with I didn't like the phrase, "took an immediate dislike to." It is one of those near-clichés. I must have been writing fast at the time and perhaps I was tired; that is why it slipped out onto the paper. Its familiar clang hit me later. Not only is it familiar, but it has a certain imprecision in its internal structure, a certain sloppiness in the use of the verb "to take," that doesn't please me personally. (Notice I say "personally." Some other writers would not be troubled by this characteristic of the phrase, and that's fine; that's *their* style.) In any case, these words were not my words. So out they went.

My next problem was to decide how I wanted to express the thought. How did I feel about the situation? What was my own, peculiar, personal way of looking at it?

One characteristic of my personal style is that sometimes, for fun, I enjoy coupling pairs of words that don't quite belong together. Editors have sometimes groused about this, but I keep doing it because it's part of my writing personality. And in this case I found a pleasant opportunity to perform the quirky little trick. I seized on the phrase, "enthusiastically disliking." The words don't quite hang together because enthusiasm is generally thought to be a component of liking, not disliking. But the odd phrase pleased *me*. These were my words, my very own.

The phrase would not necessarily please you or another writer, any more than his or your personal stylistic quirks might please me. The point is that I write as I think, not as some other writer thinks.

And so should you. That is how your style will develop its own personality.

XI

The Job to Be Done by Chapter One

The first chapter of your book is perhaps the most important chapter you will write. Other chapters may turn out to be weak, flawed, substandard in terms of the quality level of the rest of the book. Obviously you won't plan it that way and obviously you will strive to make all chapters equally good, but almost every book ever written has its weak chapter. The first chapter, however, absolutely cannot be weak. It must be among the strongest in your book, if not the strongest.

Chapter One has three important jobs to do. If it fails in any of the three, the likelihood is that the rest of the book will never be read. The three jobs are:

1. Setting the scene in terms of subject matter; telling precisely what the book is about.
2. Setting the scene in terms of your emotional attitude toward the subject matter and the emotional response you expect from the reader.
3. Hooking the reader; hinting at what is to come so that he will be drawn into the body of the book.

I think the best way for me to explain how these jobs are accomplished is to talk about some specific Chapter Ones from my own books. I don't hold up my books as models of literary virtue, but it is obviously easier for me to talk about them than about other writers' books. I know what my own problems were in writing these books, whereas I could only conjecture about the problems faced by other writers. By seeing what my problems were and how I elected to solve them, you can begin to think about ways of approaching your own Chapter Ones.

Here is how I made my Chapter Ones perform the three essential jobs:

1. Subject matter

A few years ago I wrote a book called *Casebook of a Crime Psychiatrist* (Geis). It dealt with the adventures of a New York psychiatrist, Dr. James Brussel, who had worked with the city's police in tracking down several famous criminals. Dr. Brussel's special skill was to study the *modus operandi* and other facts of an unknown criminal. From these clues he would deduce what kind of man the police should look for — including the criminal's possible physical appearance.

The title of the book gave the reader some clue as to its subject matter. Chapter One had to complete the job, define the book sharply, clearly identify the boundaries. This chapter had to say lucidly that this was to be a book of true detective-adventure tales in which a psychiatrist got inside the minds of criminals. The book, under its title, could conceivably have been a number of other things — and the first chapter had to say what it was not. It was not a book of psychiatric theory. It was not an angry book grumbling about the ways in which society breeds criminals. These might have been perfectly good books, but they were not *this* book. A reader who might have enjoyed those books might not have enjoyed this one, and vice versa. The reader had to be told instantly what he was getting into.

How? Dr. Brussel and I decided early in the project that the book should be written in the first person, as though by

him, and I first attempted to get Chapter One off the ground
by having him talk about himself:

> I am a psychiatrist, though some say not an ordinary one.
> The cases I remember most vividly have involved people I've
> never met . . .

After that beginning, I planned to have the chapter explain who Dr. Brussel was and how he worked with the
police, mentioning some of his best-known cases and talking
about his investigative methods. The actual telling of detec-
tive tales — the meat of the book — would begin with Chapter Two.

But it didn't work. Written that way, Chapter One didn't
clearly establish the nature and subject matter of the book.
Oh, sure, it *said* what the book was going to be about. It
promised the reader that he was going to get into some intriguing and exciting detective-adventure tales later on. But
it didn't present the promise convincingly. Instead of immers-
ing the reader in the subject matter, the chapter merely
danced him around it.

So I abandoned that draft. I thought, "Well, if this is a
book of adventure tales, why not start right out with an adventure tale? Why pussyfoot around? Start with a good, strong
yarn and let the reader *feel* the nature of the book right on
Page One. Save all the explaining and promising till later."

So I began a new draft by talking about one of Dr. Brussel's
most famous cases, that of the so-called "Mad Bomber." I
wrote these opening paragraphs:

> They called him the Mad Bomber. For sixteen years he had
> terrorized the City of New York by setting bombs in public
> buildings. For sixteen years the police had been trying to hunt
> him down, and in all that time they had learned nothing about
> him except that he was good at making bombs and was getting
> better every year.
> The police were desperate. They were ready to try anything,
> no matter how crazy it might seem. And so, one winter day in

1956, they came to me. They didn't really believe a psychiatrist could solve their problem, but they had run out of other ideas. They asked me, "Can you tell us anything about this kind of criminal? Anything at all that might help us?"

I knew no more about the Mad Bomber than they did. And yet, I thought, a man is reflected in his acts. If I could study the record of the man's bombings over the past sixteen years, plus whatever other clues the police had picked up, perhaps I could . . .

I quit writing at that point. I could sense I was on the wrong track again. Somehow this new Chapter One lacked the strong adventure-tale quality I wanted it to have. It sounded, instead, like the words of a man sitting in his armchair, musing, theorizing. It seemed to hint that this was going to be a book of psychiatric thoughts about criminals. Such thoughts were certainly to be part of the book, but they were not its backbone.

My error was plain. Instead of rolling up my sleeves and telling a story, I had started by telling of a man thinking about a story.

In my third attempt, I left Dr. Brussel out of the story entirely until I had it properly launched. Instead of talking about psychiatric theories, I began by talking about the Mad Bomber himself:

> The neighbors called it the Crazy House. It stood on a dreary gray street of factory workers' homes . . .

I described the neighborhood, and then I went on to talk about the mysterious man who lived in the house:

> He seemed to have no job. Once or twice a month, however, in the early mornings, neighbors would hear a metallic clanging as he opened the door of his small corrugated-iron garage. He would back out his little black Daimler, carefully close and lock the garage door after him, then drive away, not to return until evening or sometimes midnight. Where did he go? What did he do? The neighbors wondered . . .

A few pages later, I brought Dr. Brussel on stage, and throughout the chapter I alternated between sections about him and sections about the Bomber. The chapter had the quality I wanted. It clearly told the reader that he had just picked up a book of mystery-adventure stories. And that is how Chapter One finally appeared in print.

2. Attitude and response

Working on my Playboy Press book that was eventually entitled *The Very, Very Rich and How They Got That Way,* I found the basic subject matter fairly easy to define in Chapter One. The subject matter was simple and straightforward: biographies of self-made multimillionaires. It was so straightforward, in fact, that it could almost be defined by the title alone.

But Chapter One had to tell the reader something else. What was my attitude toward these biographies, and what response did I expect from the reader? Was this an angry book, grumbling about the rich as secret manipulators of government, or as oppressors of the working class, or as plunderers of natural resources? Or, conversely, was it a book that stood in awe of the very rich? And did I want the reader to take any action as a result of reading the book? Did I want him to write protesting letters to his Congressman? Did I want him to strive for wealth himself? Or was I simply asking for an emotional response: anger, awe, amusement or something else?

All these questions needed to be answered for the reader as quickly as possible after he opened the book. The need to answer them was particularly important at that point in time (the early 1970s), for a number of other books dealing with the rich were then in the bookstores. One was Ferdinand Lundberg's best seller, *The Rich and the Super-Rich,* an angry book that viewed the rich as secret manipulators of American political thought. Several others were sardonic in tone. They expressed the views of disenchanted youth, including the view that wealth is not a rewarding or useful goal toward which to aim one's life.

My task was to show the reader clearly and quickly that my book was different from these. Not that it was necessarily better; only that it was different. I was writing for a kind of reader who would probably not have been attracted to, say, Lundberg's book. I had to grab this reader by the lapels and tell him, "See, this is *your* kind of book about the rich." I had to do this in Chapter One.

It was a very short chapter — only seven pages — but I packed it densely with material calculated to show the book's attitudes and the expected response from the reader. I began with a tongue-in-cheek, almost flippant first paragraph that told the reader I didn't expect him to be awed by the wealthy:

> Come with me now, ye seekers, and stand before this great gilded door. In a while we will turn the jeweled key and go in. Step softly. Speak in whispers. You in the back there, get rid of that damned beer can. We are about to enter the presence of Wealth . . .

A couple of paragraphs later, I told the reader that this was not an angry or sarcastic book — that its attitude toward wealth was generally friendly:

> What is the purpose of our visit to this golden gallery? Why, you ask, should we study these, the immoderately rich? It is a sharp question and we must acknowledge from the start that some will say there is no sensible answer. Our quest, we will be told, is foolish. Wealth, says the 2,500-year-old platitude, is only an ephemeral thing and may not even be real at all. A man is better advised to spend his life in quest of something else. Truth, perhaps, or beauty, but not money. Money isn't worth the seeking.
>   . . . Those who [share that view] are of course welcome to come into the gallery and browse, but they will find nobody here willing to debate with them. The argument for and

against wealth is a proper subject for other times and places, but not now and not here.

I next told the reader that, while this was not essentially a book of instructions for gathering wealth, he could look upon it as such if he liked. I gave him a choice of two responses: he could read the book for plain entertainment, or he could study the lives of the rich in the hope of finding ways to become rich himself:

> With that prickly subject [the argument for and against wealth] neatly sidestepped, let's now consider what we stand to gain from our visits with the rich. For one thing we stand to be entertained. The very, very rich are an unusual and fascinating group — obviously different from you and me, as F. Scott Fitzgerald pointed out, yet not so very different that we can't see our own humanity reflected in their faces. Their stories are stories of ordinary human beings raised to stunning magnitude by forces from within and without . . .
> In a sense these are fairy tales . . . But there is a notable difference. The reader of a fairy tale cannot hope any such adventure will ever happen to him. The reader of these rich men's tales may nurture that hope — in fact, is cordially invited to do so.
> Which brings up the second good reason for our visit to this gallery. The lives of the rich men gathered here are highly instructive . . .

And so it went. The reader, by the time he reached the end of Chapter One, was thoroughly immersed in the book's attitudes. He knew not only what the subject matter was, but how I was asking him to approach it and why I was asking him to care.

3. Hooking the reader

A good Chapter One performs some of the same functions as the "tune-in-next-week" advertisement at the end of a typical television dramatic show. By giving the reader a few well-chosen hints of what is to come, a brief glimpse of an exciting scene or two, a foretaste of some intriguing bits of subject matter, you hook him.

This emphatically does not mean you should make your Chapter One into a table of contents, drily enumerating all the pieces of subject matter you are proposing to cover. That would only bore the reader. Moreover, it would probably not serve the purpose of hooking him. You hook him by arousing his curiosity, by dropping hints, by starting to say things but leaving them unfinished, so that he must read into the body of the book to get his curiosity soothed.

My book *Wall Street and Witchcraft,* for example, dealt with the use of various occult and mystical future-seeing techniques in the stock market. The temptation to make Chapter One into a table of contents was strong. I wanted to tell the reader, "Hey, come here, I've got some terrific yarns to spin about astrology, Tarot cards, ghosts, extrasensory perception, witchcraft and other weird and wonderful things. I'll tell you about a fellow who triple-quadrupled his money in six months, and another fellow who . . ."

But no. A flat, essentially emotionless checkoff of subject matter is not a reliable hook. I decided it would be much more effective to give the reader a *feeling* of the subject matter to come, rather than merely standing there flat-footed and telling him about it.

I made my Chapter One into a single long anecdote, a case study of a little white-haired man who claimed to know the stock market's future through extrasensory perception. I began by telling of a night when I went down to Wall Street to meet this odd speculator. Then I paused and dropped a hint about subject matter to come:

> I'd first heard about the old gentleman when I chanced to meet a brokerage account executive at a party. We were talking about right and wrong guesses on the stock market. The account man started to recall some clients who were right more often than seemed fair. Every brokerage house has such clients:

people who seem to possess uncanny luck or some other, unknown, maddening quality, people who always sell out just before market crashes . . .

And after a little more talk about those people, I returned
to the specific story of the little white-haired man and his
ESP. Instead of giving the reader a table of contents, I had
given him what I hoped would be (and, for a certain type of
reader, knew would be) a provocative suggestion about the
kinds of tales I was preparing to tell in future chapters.

Similarly, in my *Very Rich* book, I didn't list the entire
cast of characters in Chapter One. I mentioned just two of
the men whose biographies were to appear later in the book.
I remarked that J. Paul Getty, the oil billionaire, is so fabu-
lously rich that he honestly doesn't know how much money
he has. And I mentioned the intriguing air of secrecy that
surrounds Howard Hughes. I figured those two mentions
would be enough to show the reader that the very rich are
unusual people, and to arouse his curiosity.

In another part of that same Chapter One, I made just
one more brief promise about material to come. I wanted the
reader to know that the book wasn't confined to strictly biographical stories, that there were other kinds of material to
pique his curiosity. In a section where I was talking about the
high risks assumed by most of the great capitalists, I made my
promise like this:

> It should be pointed out that these high-stakes games pro-
> duce losers as well as winners. We have collected only the win-
> ners here. Nobody knows the losers' names. It is interesting to
> speculate about the reasons for winning and losing: why one
> man goes up while another man, starting out on the same
> route in substantially the same way, goes down. Character has
> something to do with it, and so does plain luck. We will study
> both these phenomena in the course of our visit.

Notice that I didn't tell the reader whether character is

more important than luck, or how each operates, or anything else. I simply left such questions hanging in the air. To resolve them, the reader would have to finish the book.

XII

BE SPECIFIC!

Be specific! This is one of the commandments of the nonfiction book writing business, and it may even be the *first* commandment. It is also the one most often broken by beginning writers.

Generalities are the products of lazy thinking, lazy research and lazy writing. Generalities have no force — no power to persuade, to stir up, to produce either intellectual or emotional responses. And perhaps worst of all, generalities are totally uninteresting as reading matter.

Here is a generality: "More people like dogs than like cats." Even in casual conversation, such a statement would be both dull and unconvincing. In writing, it would be unacceptable. *The general must always be supported by the specific.*

There are three main ways in which this can be done. The general statement can be supported by facts and figures, by quotes from people who can be considered authorities on the subject, or by anecdotes. Let's see how this might work out in the case of that generality about dogs and cats.

Facts and figures. You might dig up a formal survey on the subject, and in that case the generality would become specific like this: "According to a survey made last year by the XYZ Opinion Research Center of Ivy University, 78% of adults say they are fond of dogs, while only 62% profess any liking for cats . . ."

The generality has now become convincing and is beginning to become interesting. It can be made still more interesting by adding still more specific material — by following it, for example, with a quote or anecdote or both.

Quotes. You might find a pet dealer who is willing to be quoted on the subject, or the editor of a magazine devoted to pets, or perhaps an official in a government bureau that concerns itself with domestic animals. The quotable person could be anybody, as long as you can show in identifying him that he is an authority on this particular subject.

Your statement might then go like this: "According to Joe Smith, owner of Smith's Pet Store in Small City, Arkansas, dog fanciers outnumber cat fanciers by a wide margin — at least in his experience. 'In an average week,' says Smith, 'I get dozens of people in here looking to buy dogs . . .' "

And so on. Smith's statement doesn't actually prove the generality in the same sense that the XYZ opinion survey proves it. Instead, Smith's statement supports it — lends it a degree of credibility which it wouldn't have if it were simply left to stand as a flat generality in the writer's words.

It isn't always necessary to *prove* a generality as though you were defending it in a court of law. You need only support it, give your reader some logical reason for paying attention to it. If you find you can't actually prove a generality, you can always reword it to make it into a less dogmatic statement. Instead of saying flatly that "more people like dogs," for example, you can say, "At least in Joe Smith's experience . . ."

Anecdotes. To lend another kind of support to that statement about dogs and cats, you can tell a story that illustrates the point. The story might begin:

Joe Smith, the pet store man, recalls a day last winter when a dog fell through the ice on a pond in Small City Park. Hundreds of people gathered around the edge of the pond, giving advice and shouting encouragement to a gallant team of police and firemen who turned out to rescue the dog. A passing caterer's truck stopped to dispense hot coffee . . .

By contrast, hardly anybody paid any attention when a cat got itself stranded on top of a Revolutionary War monument in the same park that same winter . . .

Notice again that the anecdote does not actually prove the generality. The anecdote only supports it. That is usually enough.

And notice one other thing that is of paramount importance. The anecdote makes the generality interesting. It adds color, life, bounce. Without this kind of support, the generality is not worth reading.

Now let's see how specific facts, quotes, and anecdotes can be handled in the actual writing of a nonfiction book. For simplicity I'll talk about one of my own books, *The Weekenders* (Lippincott) , a study of what Americans do on weekends and why. The subject mattter of this book was somewhat amorphous, and for that reason I was obliged to work doubly hard to pin my statements down with specifics. I was strongly aware, throughout the project, that many readers would approach the book skeptically and would be inclined not to swallow any of it unless I supported it strongly all the way.

There are three useful ways of linking a generality with its supporting specifics. Using examples picked at random from *The Weekenders,* I'll illustrate the three approaches one by one.

1. Generalizing into the specific. You begin by stating the generality you want to put across, and then you follow it with supporting facts, quotes or anecdotes.

In one section of *The Weekenders,* I was trying to show

that weekend life in America is not always serene, as leisure time is supposed to be, but often becomes just the opposite. I supported the generality with a quote, like this:

> . . . Peace is nowhere in the weekend picture — or, if it is there, lies somewhere in a corner obscured by dust and turmoil. The weekenders golf, ski, bowl and boat. They dance, tell jokes and make love. They drink standing up and sitting down. They go to theaters, art galleries and concerts. They play with their children, go to church and sell dented brass candlestick holders at PTA bazaars. They build things, repair things, paint things and plant things. Many a business official has said he'd be pleased if the weekday people threw themselves into their work with half that much spirit. Lemuel Boulware put it succinctly when he was vice-president and personnel chief of General Electric. "It is not this company's policy," said he plaintively, "to send people home on Friday as tired as they come in on Monday."

In another part of the same chapter, still trying to make my point about the fast pace of weekend life, I used the same technique of generalizing into the specific. This time, the supporting specifics were in the form of statistical facts:

> Weekend traffic has a brittle, aggressive quality. The weekenders are irritable, easily angered, easily tempted into high-horsepower foolishness . . . They have more accidents than anybody. The National Safety Council says an average Tuesday or Wednesday in 1960 saw 81 deaths in automobile accidents across the nation. But an average Friday saw 110, an average Saturday 154 and an average Sunday 125.

2. *Generalizing out of the specific.* You present your specific data, quote or anecdote first, and then you sum it up by drawing a general inference from it.

At one point in *The Weekenders* I was trying to demonstrate that Americans' attitudes toward work — the status conveyed by a job, the work-week feeling of being needed and useful — sometimes prevent them from enjoying free time as fully as possible. I opened the discussion with an anecdote, like this:

> Dr. Alexander Reid Martin, chairman of the American Psychiatric Association's Standing Committee on Leisure Time and Its Uses, has spent much of his professional life studying people's reactions to what he calls "unstructured time." One of his patients, he recalls, was a business executive with a gastric ulcer. Every Friday evening as the work-week neared its end, the man suffered acute pain. The pain diminished somewhat when he went home but recurred in spasms throughout the weekend. On Mondays, the pain went away. Once he tried to take a vacation. The thought of several weeks' unstructured time produced gastric agony so intolerable that he went to a hospital instead.
>
> Nearly all people in our society need work to hang their lives upon. Some need it more than others. Some need it so badly that when work is snatched away their lives start to disintegrate . . .

3. *Making the specific imply the general.* You present your specific facts, quotes, or anecdotes, and you let it go at that. You don't state the implied generality. You let the reader draw that inference for himself.

In a chapter entitled "The Weekend Intelligentsia," I was making some points about the practice, common among upper-middle-class suburbanites, of force-feeding culture to themselves and other people. I told a story about the Shakespeare Festival at Stratford, Connecticut:

> Patrons of the theater were . . . baffled by the stage background against which the plays were performed. Instead of ordinary scenery there was non-scenery made of odd crinkly-textured shapes. Except for the neutral color, these shapes looked exactly like huge potato chips. Seeking to show the esthetic reasoning behind this, the Festival's program booklet explained that it was a "curving, plastic continuum. Essentially, it is a sliced-through invisible dome, suggesting a complete atmospheric surround, with neither beginning nor end . . ."
>
> One hot Saturday night at intermission time, as the crowd

milled around outdoors, a man's voice was heard protesting loudly. "I've had all the culture I can take!" he howled. "Used to be, I couldn't understand what I came to see. Now I can't even understand the damned program!"

I suppose I could have preceded or followed this little story with a generality. I could have pointed out that culture is a waste of time if you don't enjoy it, or I could have asked why people feel socially pressured to visit cultural events in which they aren't really interested. But this general statement on my part seemed unnecessary. The story made its own point. It seemed like more fun, to me, to let the reader draw his own generalized conclusions.

There is just one last truth I would like to leave with you. The specific can stand by itself, without any support from the general. But vice versa? Never.

XIII

FICTIONAL TECHNIQUES IN NONFICTION WRITING

When you write a nonfiction book, it should not contain fiction disguised as fact. If you tell an anecdote and represent it to be true, it should be true. If you quote somebody, the quoted person should actually have said what you say he said. These are major commandments of the nonfiction writing business.

It is obvious that some writers break these commandments, and a few break them consistently. It is possible, even easy, to invent an anecdote or make up a quote. It is done simply by writing anecdotes or quotes "blind" — that is, failing to identify the people involved. Instead of saying "Joe Smith, police chief of Smallville, Texas," the writer says "a police chief of a small southern town." Since nobody knows who the police chief is (or even whether he exists except in the writer's imagination), the writer feels at liberty to make up stories about him or to quote words that were never actually spoken.

Sometimes a true anecdote or a genuine quote must be written blind. This happens most often when you are dealing with a delicate or prickly subject. People you interview will request that their names not appear in print, and you are bound by reportorial honor (and also by the fear of lawsuits) to respect their wishes. Yes. You can write blind quotes and anecdotes as long as you don't lose credibility by writing too many close together. A reader will accept a certain amount of blind material in a nonfiction book, provided the bulk of the book has a strong aura of truth. But if you value your reputation as a journalist and look forward to a long and successful nonfiction career, you should never tell a story that didn't happen or quote words that weren't spoken.

Why not? On the surface, it might seem that a blind anecdote would sound the same to the reader whether it is true or not. How can the reader tell whether the "police chief of a small southern town" exists, or whether this police chief did or didn't become involved in a certain adventure?

My answer is that I don't know exactly how the reader can tell — *but somehow, he can.* Perhaps he might be fooled by the first two or three pieces of blind material in a book, but he will not remain fooled for long. Sooner or later there will come a time when he begins to suspect he is being lied to. He is bothered, perhaps, by the paucity of detail in the writer's fictitious anecdotes — the kinds of detail that always surround real-life stories and that can't be successfully invented (except perhaps by the most skillful fiction writers — and I'm not even sure they can do it consistently well). Or perhaps the invented details don't quite fit together convincingly. Or perhaps the faked quotes lack the easy rhythm or spontaneity of real colloquial speech. At any rate, every normal reader recognizes the ring of truth when he hears it and recognizes its lack when it is not there. So does every good editor.

Faked nonfiction books are published from time to time. They seldom go anywhere. Their writers, meagerly paid because the market does not value their work very highly, quickly vanish into obscurity. They are forced to turn to other lines of work, for in time they discover that the pay scale for their brand of writing will never go any higher than rock bottom.

Yet there is a place for fictional techniques in good nonfiction writing. You can feel free to fictionalize in certain situations where such an approach is warranted — and in fact you should welcome the opportunity when it comes around, for fictional techniques can add a good deal of life and color to a nonfiction book.

The main rule to observe is this: be honest with your reader. Whenever you depart from strict factual reporting and drift into more imaginative treatments of your material — drift toward fiction — be sure you tell the reader what you are doing. Don't ever try to sell him fiction in the clothing of fact.

As an example of a semifictional approach to factual material, consider *The Split-Level Trap* (Geis), a book that I wrote in collaboration with psychiatrist Dr. Richard Gordon. The meat of this book was a gallery of case histories illustrating emotional problems among suburbanites. The case histories were drawn from Dr. Gordon's files. However, medical ethics forbade us to reveal the identities of the doctor's patients. To avoid lawsuits, we were obliged to use fictitious names and to disguise the stories fairly heavily.

We took care to tell the readers what we were doing. In an introductory chapter we explained:

> . . . No case was drawn entirely from any one family or person, but each represents some of the situations, problems and personality types most commonly handled in a suburban psychiatric practice. If any characteristic in these cases reminds the reader of traits in himself, the coincidence is of course intentional.

Later in the book, we paused once in a while in the middle of a story to remind the reader we were using a semifictional approach. For example, one case study opened like this:

> In a corner of a dark bedroom closet, in a three-year-old split-level house, a young wife crouched like a small, frightened animal. Her husband pleaded with her to tell him what was troubling her, but she would not speak. She stared out at him fearfully . . .

The story of Alice Hager (as we will call her) illustrates some of the emotional stresses that bear on young married women in a mobile society . . .

That little phrase in parentheses was our reminder to the reader that we were drifting away from literal fact. A woman such as Alice Hager actually existed, but her name was not Alice Hager, her house was not three years old, and the closet in which her husband found her was not a bedroom closet.

In writing that book, I was acutely concerned about losing the ring of truth amid all our fictionalizing. To preserve the ring of truth, we wedged sections of strictly factual reporting in between the case histories — including some deliberately dry statistical material — and we assured the reader of our honesty by telling him what we were doing at all times. By using devices such as the parenthetical note about Alice Hager's name, we clearly labeled our semifictional passages as such. As a result, the book held together as a work of nonfiction. It was condensed in a major women's magazine, sold nicely in the hardcover edition, and became a best seller in paperback. Some critics complained about the psychiatric theories advanced in the book, and others complained about other things, but nobody said he found the case stories unbelievable.

The fear of lawsuits — the need to protect people's privacy — is only one of the reasons why a nonfiction writer must sometimes stray into semifiction. An equally good reason is that, in certain situations, the fictional technique simply makes for a more colorful and interesting treatment of the material at hand.

This happens most commonly when you are faced with the need to describe a scene or episode you didn't witness and patently couldn't have witnessed. For example, consider a problem I faced in writing *Casebook of a Crime Psychiatrist*. This book described the experiences of a psychiatric criminologist, Dr. James Brussel, and was written in the first person as though by Dr. Brussel. One of his cases involved the 1963 murder of two New York career girls, Janice Wylie and Emily Hoffert. The case has never been solved to everyone's satisfaction, including Dr. Brussel's. Studying the clues surrounding this bizarre, incredibly gory crime, Dr. Brussel formed a clear mental picture of the killer, his actions and his motives. My problem, in writing up the case, was to present Dr. Brussel's speculations in an interesting way.

I first tried to present them straightforwardly, as speculations. I wrote:

> It seemed to me that he was probably a young man, most likely in the two girls' age bracket. I doubted that his motive was burglary, for no other apartment in the building had been entered and there were no reports of a prowler or anybody else going from door to door. This man had apparently gone straight to the two girls' apartment, ignoring some much bigger apartments and richer tenants on other floors. It is likely that he knocked on the door, for there is no evidence that the door was forced or the lock picked. He must have been a pleasant-looking man, neatly dressed, for the girls invited him in . . .

Then I thought, *no, there's a better way.* The straightforward approach was somewhat dry. Moreover, it was confusing and promised to grow more so. The complex chain of thought could be presented much more colorfully *and more clearly* through a fictional approach. So I did it like this:

> I thought about the puzzle when the lieutenant left. I had already formed a picture of the killer. Now I began to form a tentative picture of his actions. I saw him . . .
> A young man, impeccably dressed, carrying an attaché case: the perfect young urban sophisticate . . . It is noon. He stands on the sidewalk of East Eighty-eighth Street, watching the door of Janice Wylie's apartment building. He is waiting for the doorman to leave his post . . .

And I went on from there to give a long, detailed fictionalized account of the crime as Dr. Brussel reconstructed it.

Since it was obvious that Dr. Brussel could not have witnessed the crime, there could be no doubt in the reader's mind that this was something other than straight factual reporting. The reader knew he was into a passage of semifiction. Yet the fictional technique did no damage to the aura of truth. In fact it enhanced the truth — the complex bundle of thoughts in the doctor's head — by clarifying it.

Just as it is possible to write a novel based on a core of fact, so it is possible to write a nonfiction book with occasional patches of fiction. There are some purists in the literary world who object to such hybridization, as they call it. As for me, I like it. The two great breeds of literary craftsmanship, fiction and nonfiction, are not really that dissimilar, after all. They are complementary rather than mutually exclusive. Each can impart color, force, and clarity to the other. In the right places at the right times, they can live together very happily.

XIV

FINDING A GOOD TITLE

When you submit a book manuscript to an editor, you can quite safely assume that your title will vanish somewhere along the route from here to publication. *The Split-Level Trap* is the only book title of my own that ever appeared in print. Another title stayed alive but got turned back-to-front: I'd proposed *Witchcraft on Wall Street,* but an editor changed it to *Wall Street and Witchcraft,* partly to gain some obscure advantage in library indexing procedures. Not one of my other titles has ever survived in recognizable form. And my record — one-and-a-half surviving titles — seems to be a pretty good one. Many nonfiction book writers lament that they have never conceived a title that lived.

I say "lament," but I don't really mean that. Many editors are good at inventing titles — and that is one reason why publishers pay their salaries. A minor reason, perhaps, but a sound one, for the title begins the process of selling the book to the readers. Nearly every major publishing house has at least one editor who is considered especially clever with titles, and the other editors go to him or her whenever they find themselves holding a good book without a good name.

By contrast, nonfiction writers as a breed rarely seem to master this peculiar knack of book titling. Perhaps this is because the writer has lived with his book and its ideas too long, and he has lost the capacity to condense it into the tiny package of a title.

Thus it is unlikely that any title of yours will make it to the printing press. Despite this, you should still try to come up with a workmanlike title. Even though you and the editors consider it tentative and ephemeral, it is still useful. It has some jobs to do.

For one thing, a good title will help you focus your thoughts while you are working on the book. It will help you pull together what might otherwise be an unwieldy mass of material that is trying to flow in all directions at once. It will help you decide what material to discard, how to shape and aim the material you keep, which research routes to explore and which to ignore. In working on *Wall Street and Witchcraft,* for example, I kept hearing about certain self-styled witches, astrologers and other occultists who sounded like fascinating people. Being curious by nature and trade — an incurable reporter — I was strongly tempted to go out and interview these odd and appealing folk. But my title, even in its back-to-front form, kept me solidly on the track. The book was about occultists operating *on Wall Street.* No matter how fascinating an occult practitioner might be, if he had nothing to do with the stock market he had nothing to do with my book.

Another good reason why you should develop a workmanlike title is that your book, in its early faltering stages, will need a convenient handle by which people can mentally grab it. The author's tentative title is usually called the "working title," for it is a title to work with. Not only for you to work with, but for the editors, too.

Generally, you start by sending a query letter to a publishing house, followed by sample chapters and an outline if the response is favorable. Ideally there should be a tentative title in the initial query, but if you can't think of one at that stage, you should invent a title at least by the time you reach the sample-chapters-and-outline stage. For if the proposed book has any appeal at all to the editors, they will now begin talking about it among themselves — and they will go on talking about it, thinking about it, writing memos about it, all during the long months when you are researching and writing the final manuscript.

What should they call it? "That book about those crazy folks who try to predict the stock market with — um — astrology and stuff like that"? No, they need something more specific. From your point of view, the working title — even though tentative and probably doomed to die — should be a good, lively, descriptive title that will do its own share of selling in those editorial conversations and memos. It should be a title which by its nature makes the book sound intriguing and predisposes editors to talk about it favorably.

What makes a good title? The suggestions that follow are only that; they are not rules. Any title-writing "rule" can be broken, and indeed has been broken many times in the final titles of successful books. But as a beginner you are probably wiser to stick with what is accepted and safe than to experiment too ambitiously. It is true of all skills, including writing, that an expert can break rules because his experience has taught him precisely how and when he can do so profitably. A beginner, lacking that experience, should tread more warily. These suggestions will make your title, if not brilliant, at least satisfactory:

1. Keep it brief — if possible, six words or less. I know there have been best sellers with much longer titles. I've seen this rule broken with some of my own books, notably *The Very, Very Rich and How They Got That Way*. But as a general truth, shorter titles are more likely to capture people's imaginations (editors' and readers' alike) than long ones.

If you want evidence of this, look at any nonfiction bestseller list, any month, any week. I can virtually guarantee that the average word length of the titles will be six or less

— far less some weeks, when the average may drop as low as three per title. If the best-seller lists are reliable indicators, it would seem that editors and book buyers alike are attracted to short titles.

If you are a beginner, your safest course is to play along with the averages. If most editors like short titles most of the time, don't risk annoying them with a long title.

2. Make it describe the book. This rule-that-isn't-a-rule is broken much more often than the one about brevity. Among books currently on the nonfiction best-seller lists as I write this are *The Game of the Foxes, The Boys of Summer* and *I'm O.K. — You're O.K.* Not one of these titles says clearly what the book is about. But remember that what you are composing is a working title designed as much for its usefulness to you and the editors as for its flash and glitter. Your title should give at least some hint about the book's subject matter. A mystifying or seemingly irrelevant title may only irritate the editors to whom you submit the book. They will think, "Oh, the author is just showing off."

Later, they may publish your book with a mystifying title of their own. But that is their fun. Let them have it.

3. Make it lively and interesting. Don't be satisfied with a drab, flat, descriptive title like the label on a file folder. When I was first thinking about my book, *Wall Street and Witchcraft* — before I submitted the idea to any publisher — the title I scribbled on the file folder in which I started collecting material was *Wall Street — Occult Arts.* This obviously didn't have it as a title. An editor glancing at it would be predisposed to expect a dull book. It was necessary for me to play with the title for a while, kick at it, prod it, add to it, subtract from it, take it apart, turn it this way and that. I wanted a title that would express the liveliness of the book I felt growing in my head.

There are absolutely no rules I can give you for making a title lively, appealing, eye-catching and ear-catching. It is a matter of seeking artful ways to express a thought — sometimes more than one thought — in a strictly limited number of words. You simply have to spend some time, perhaps weeks, turning the possibilities over and over in your mind. Try alliteration. Try rhyme. Try a clever and unexpected twist on some shopworn old phrase. Sit down with a dictionary or thesaurus and seek synonyms for the words that have crossed your mind. Talk about it with your husband, wife, kids, friends. One of them may come up with a felicitous phrase. Or you may surprise yourself: the phrase may suddenly jump from your own mouth when you least expect it.

Do not despair if the right title — short, descriptive, lively — eludes you at first. You can write your initial query letter, if you have to, without having a working title to suggest. As long as the query is good and the basic idea sound, the lack of a title probably will not damage your case.

If the editors like the query and encourage you to submit an outline and sample chapters, you will then be obliged to compose a title during that second stage. But the frustrating little chore may abruptly become easier.

Go ahead and write your sample chapters and your outline. It is highly likely that your missing title will appear before you, like a genie, as you write. Some phrase that you use in the text of the book, or some odd little clump of words that flits through your mind as you pore over your research will suddenly jump up at you. You will recognize it instantly. It will have been lurking in the back of your mind, not quite visible, for days or weeks. It will be your title.

XV

Putting It All Together

A good nonfiction book is not just a sheaf of chapters, loosely tied together by having some general relevance to the same subject. Ideally, a book is a single unit, a whole.

This ideal is not always easy to achieve, for a number of practical problems get in the writer's way. Although he wants his book to be a single unit, he must of course build it out of separate parts, written separately. If he could write the entire book in a single day, working straight through from page one to the end, it would flow together naturally as a unit. But no such working method is possible. It takes anywhere from a couple of months to a couple of years to write a book. The writer may work on the chapters out of their final numerical order. His mood when he is writing one chapter may be different from his mood when writing another, so that the two chapters emerge with different sounds and attitudes. The ongoing research may change his mind about certain aspects of the subject matter, so that the last few chapters he writes display a bias not present in the first few. And in the course of the work, he may simply grow as a writer. The last third of the book may be written in a more highly developed, more personal style than the first third.

How do you tie a book together so that it becomes a whole?

The first piece of advice I would give you is that you write the entire book in rough draft before starting to clean-type any of it. Once you do the final typing of any chapter, you lock that chapter up. Even though you decide later that the chapter really ought to be changed, you are reluctant to make the changes because this will necessitate retyping. Don't type yourself into a corner that way. Leave everything in rough-draft form — changeable, flexible — until the entire book says what you want it to say. Then, and only then, start the clean-typing process.

The sample chapters you submitted earlier in the game, when you were in the process of selling your book, can also be considered changeable. No editor will ever complain if you tell him you want to rewrite those chapters, improve them, bring them into line with your subsequent thinking and research. The editor knows how books are written, and he knows what the problems are. He is aware that the last half of a book, as it is being written, can throw new light on what has already been said in the first half. He doesn't consider your sample chapters to be locked up, and he will not hold you to them.

For the same reasons, he will make no complaints if you deviate from your original outline — provided, of course, that your reasons are sound. The outline is not a formal contract, to be obeyed word-for-word. As long as the final book is substantially what your samples and outline promised it would be, nobody will object if some of your chapters appear in a different order from that indicated in the outline, or if some new chapters are added, or if some elements of subject matter are omitted because they turned out to be less useful than you thought at first.

When you have finished the rough draft of your book, let it lie fallow for a week. Turn your thoughts to something else. Go to movies. Watch television. Read other books — but not books that have anything to do with your book's subject matter. Obviously, it will be impossible to forget your own book, but do the best you can.

Then pick up your rough draft and read it straight

through, quickly. Don't try to do any editing at this time. Just make notes to yourself on the margins when you come across anything that needs work. Ask yourself whether the book "tracks" — whether each chapter flows smoothly and logically into the next. Does the book fulfill the promises made and implied in the first chapter? Are any changes of attitude evident as the book progresses? Any shifts of emphasis, any inconsistencies that will leave the reader wondering what you really mean?

Also ask yourself whether the chapters are in the right order. Does Chapter Four contain some material that would come across more strongly or clearly if it were preceded by Chapter Five?

Pay special attention to clarity. The material is perfectly clear to you because you've been living with it all these months. But will it be perfectly clear to the reader? I always find several passages of unclear material in my own rough drafts. The sheer size of the writing project, the sheer length of time over which I've worked on it, makes this almost unavoidable. I may have written Chapter Eight before Chapter Six, for example, because of the way my research material happened to flow in. In Chapter Eight I may have included material that needed some kind of background, some pre-explanation, perhaps some emotional preparation for the reader. I planned to put this necessary foundation into Chapter Six — but when I finally got around to writing Chapter Six a month later, I forgot all the clever thoughts I was thinking while writing Chapter Eight.

Also watch for unnecessary repetition. This, again, is an ailment that springs from the sheer length of the project. Writing Chapter Eight, you are tempted to repeat something you said in Chapter Two. You dimly remember having said it, but you think, "Well, that was weeks ago; the reader has forgotten it by now." For the reader, however, it was probably only an hour or a day ago. He has not forgotten it, and the repetition will only irritate him.

Having gone through your draft quickly, sit down with your typewriter and a pencil and go through it a second time, slowly. Make all the larger changes you determined should be made during your first read-through. And this time, pay close attention to writing style.

You are likely to find, perhaps to your delight, that your style improved markedly in the last half of the book. This probably happened largely because you became more comfortable with the subject matter. You were able to write about it more authoritatively, more smoothly. A certain hesitation and jerkiness was probably apparent in Chapter One, but it is gone by the time you reach the midsection of the book.

You can now lift some strong stylistic elements from your later chapters and salt them into your early chapters. Often this can be done with a pencil, though you may find you need to run some passages through your typewriter.

What kinds of stylistic changes will these be? For one thing, you will probably notice that, in the latter half of the book, you have developed what my wife calls "felicitous phrases." (It amuses her that, whenever I invent such a phrase, I tend to walk around mumbling it to myself.) Such phrases describe or refer to certain complicated concepts that recur throughout the book. In the first few chapters, you had difficulty in writing about these concepts; you couldn't think of the right words. But as the work progressed and you became more at home with your subject, you began to work out clearer, stronger, shorter ways to express these difficult thoughts.

As an example, consider a problem I wrestled with in *Wall Street and Witchcraft*. In the early chapters, I couldn't think of a good way to describe people who use occult and mystical pseudosciences to play the stock market. I tried all kinds of phrases, including the one I've just used: "people who use occult and mystical pseudosciences . . ." I tried awkward hyphenated phrases such as "occult-using speculators." I tried "market occultists" and half a dozen other labels.

Later in the book, I warmed up to my topic. I relaxed with it. And somewhere around Chapter Five, I began talking about "rational" market-playing techniques, as opposed to the occult and mystical ones. The obverse of that word gave me the phrase I wanted: "the irrationals." I used that phrase through the remainder of the book.

When I read through my rough draft, I saw how hesitant and uncomfortable my early chapters were. I lifted my felicitous phrase out of Chapter Five. With my typewriter and scissors and a paste pot, I inserted it into Chapter Two with an introduction like this:

> Why does one man win on the stock market while another man loses? Some would say it is because the winner has a clever technique . . . or simply because he is lucky. This would be the rational explanation. . . . But there are other explanations which, for want of a better word, I'll call irrational. I don't necessarily use the word in its derogatory sense . . .

Having pasted this into my draft, I then went through the rest of the early chapters and penciled in "the irrationals" wherever I had used a longer, weaker, more awkward phrase.

Such stylistic changes have the effect of tying the book together, making it feel more like a whole. In some cases, the changes will be broader than mere improvements of phrasing. You may find that your attitude toward your subject, your feelings about it, have changed subtly as you neared the end of your book — and that these changed feelings have somehow colored your writing. Your task then will be to identify these feelings — sort them out, if you can — and spread them through your early chapters.

Reading the rough draft of *The Weekenders,* for instance,

I was struck by a certain warmth in the last chapters, a kind of lilt in the writing style, that was lacking in the early chapters. The early chapters seemed dry and stilted as I read them over — though I had been happy with them when I first wrote them. This puzzled me, for I couldn't immediately spot any tangible differences. It finally came to me that my whole spectrum of emotional attitudes toward the book had shifted somewhere in the middle of the project.

I had begun by thinking of it as a kind of light-hearted sociological report, a straightforward journalistic study of what people do on weekends and why. Somewhere near the middle, I lost my journalistic detachment and became more emotional. I began talking more often of the glorious fun a weekend offers, provided the weekender doesn't let it get cluttered with real or imagined obligations. I began talking of "leisure" as something to be loved and treasured, rather than using the word as a mere adjective to describe a span of time or a type of merchandise. More and more often as the book progressed, I found myself using words like "idyll" and "festival" when I meant "weekend."

All this came home to me as I pondered my rough draft. Somehow, I saw, I had to infuse the first chapters with this sense of warmth and gaiety.

I began with the very first paragraph of Chapter One. That chapter had originally begun:

> The weekend begins some time around noon on Friday. All over America at that hour, life seems to gather momentum . . .

A journalistic report — dry, detached. Perfectly good and workmanlike, but the mood of the last chapters was lacking. The book was not whole. Chapter One seemed not to have been written by the same man who wrote Chapter Twelve.

To instill Chapter One with the emotional tone or mood of the last chapters, I wrote a whole new first paragraph, leading into the original first paragraph like this:

> Some people hold celebrations to honor gods and spirits. We
> hold one every week to honor leisure. We call it the weekend.
> So hang up the bright ribbons and uncork the festive jug. Close
> the file cabinet, still the loud machine, bank the weekday fires.
> Let dour work now hide his ugly face. For this is the time when
> joy may come among us again.
> The festival lasts two days but the mood precedes it. The
> mood begins to be felt sometime around noon on Friday. All
> over America at that hour . . .

I made similar changes at a number of other places in my
early chapters, some with typed inserts, some with a pencil.
When I was finished, the emotional quality I had developed
in the last chapters pervaded the entire book. I am still not
perfectly satisfied with the way I handled the problem, but
the book did seem to come out of the operation as a single
unit.

I once heard an editor say that wholeness in a book "is
something like love. Nobody can quite define it. But when
you've got it, you *know* you've got it."

Moreover, it satisfies.

XVI

WRITER TO WRITER: SOME QUESTIONS AND ANSWERS

Can I sell my book more easily through an agent?

Probably not. In the first place, as a beginner, you won't easily find a good agent who is willing to take you on. As a general rule, an agent depends on commissions for his income. If he sells nothing, he earns nothing. Obviously it would be a risk for him to take on beginners whose abilities he cannot judge. He prefers established professionals with proven track records.

In the second place, there is no assurance that an agent could sell your work any more easily than you can. Your book will be bought or rejected on the basis of what you submit to publishers: your idea, your query, your outline, your final manuscript. If these are good, they'll find a home. If they aren't, they won't — whether you are agented or not.

Literary folklore has it that editors pay close attention to queries and manuscripts submitted through agents, while ignoring those that come in "over the transom" from unknown beginners. This may be true in some branches of the writing business, but not in the nonfiction book business. Editors are paid to seek out printable manuscripts, and they seek wherever they think the treasure might be — including each day's mail.

What are agents for, then?
An agent can be highly valuable to a professional book writer who gets involved in book club sales, movie sales, and the sale of other subsidiary rights. For you, that can come later.

How should queries, outlines and manuscripts be typed?
A query can be single-spaced, like an ordinary letter — on one side of the paper only, of course. Anything longer than seven or eight pages ought to be double-spaced for easy reading. This includes your sample chapters and, of course, the final book manuscript.

Start each new chapter about a third of the way down the page. This leaves space at the top for editors' notes. Be sure your typewriter ribbon is new enough to type in solid black, not gray. Editors must plow through huge amounts of reading material, and at the end of a long day their eyes are tired. Dim manuscripts annoy them.

Will it hurt my chances if I'm not a perfect typist?
No, as long as your manuscript is reasonably neat. A couple of typing errors per page won't hurt — if corrections are penciled in before the manuscript is submitted. However, every page should be perfectly legible. Don't smother your pages with penciled inserts.

How should queries and manuscripts be mailed?
A query can be mailed like a letter, folded in three. The manuscript is better mailed flat. The sample-chapters-and-outline package will probably fit into a 9 x 12 Manila envelope comfortably, so you can either put it into a ream-size typewriter paper box or put it between two flat pieces of cardboard held with rubber bands. Then wrap the package in

extra strong brown paper and tie it securely with stout twine before mailing it. The U. S. Post Office is not noted for its gentleness with manuscripts.

Post Office regulations permit a manuscript to be mailed very cheaply, in the category of "educational materials." However, the regulations also say that the Post Office may take its time about delivering such mail. Use the cheap service, and your manuscript may sit for weeks at the bottom of a handcart somewhere, perhaps bent double under several tons of other mail. My advice: use first-class mail. It isn't that expensive, after all. As a rule of thumb, figure on roughly a dollar per hundred manuscript pages. Isn't your precious book worth a few dollars?

After mailing my material, how long should I expect to wait before I hear from the publisher?

Most publishers will respond to an initial query within four weeks. The response to a sample-chapters-and-outline package may take as long as eight weeks, for at this stage the editors must decide whether to offer you a formal book contract and under what terms. This requires a good deal of thought and discussion on their part. As for a final manuscript, the response time can vary from a few days (the editor was eager to read it) to several months (he can't decide whether he likes it) .

Whatever you do, give the editors the time they must have. Be patient. If you've waited six or eight weeks and have heard no word, write a very brief, friendly note asking whether the editors have yet reached a decision. Don't be prickly about it, don't scold the editors for their tardiness, and, above all, don't try to hurry them by pretending other publishers are clamoring to see your manuscript. No editor older than twenty-one ever believes that story.

If I sell my book, will the publisher reimburse me for travel and phone expenses incurred during the research?
No.

If I sell the book, how will I be paid?
The basic form of payment in the book business is the royalty: a percentage of the book's retail price. The standard royalty is 10%. That is, if the book sells for $5 a copy, you get 50¢ for each copy sold. This standard royalty is subject to nearly limitless variations, exceptions, ifs, and buts. A beginner selling his first book is most likely to be offered the standard 10%, no more, no less.

Is there any way to estimate how many copies of a given book might be sold? Can the author ever guess how much money he'll make?
No.

In other words, I might risk a year of time to write a book, and maybe sell three copies and make a buck and a half. Wouldn't that be a foolish gamble?
Not necessarily. If you have a sound idea and have learned your writing craft well, a publisher may be willing to share the risk with you. He may offer you what is called an "advance against royalties." This is a payment that he makes to you — usually in installments — while you are writing the book. When the book is published, you get no further money until the royalties credited to you have exceeded the advance. In this sense the advance is something like a loan. However, it is unlike a loan in that it is non-returnable. If your book fails to earn the advance, you don't have to refund the difference to the publisher. The advance is yours to keep. Through this mechanism, the publisher shares your risk.

An advance can be almost any amount, from a couple of hundred dollars up into the high thousands. Indeed, blockbuster books have sometimes fetched advances of more than $100,000. But very, very few writers ever hit a jackpot of that size. As a first-time book writer, your primary goal is to get your book published. Your first published book becomes a stepping-stone to your second, your third and others beyond. Don't be too much concerned with money this first time. Consider it a necessary apprenticeship.

If I'm writing an angry book in which I criticize people or organizations by name, what should I know about libel laws?

You need know only a few basic facts. The editor who works on your book will be thoroughly familiar with libel law and will carefully examine sections of the book that he feels are potentially libelous. In addition, every publishing company retains a law firm or employs a staff lawyer to check manuscripts for troublesome material. If you are worried about any particular passage in your book, make a point of calling the editor's attention to that passage and ask him to study it with extra care. He will appreciate your caution. He doesn't want a libel suit any more than you do.

Libel is defined as published slander. If you print or broadcast a false, malicious statement that does injury to somebody's personal, professional or business life, or that similarly injures an organization, that is libel, and the injured party has a right to sue you for damages in a court of law. Chances are he won't, for it costs a lot of money to mount such a suit. He may only grumble at you. Still, there is no point in taking needless risks — and in any case, legal questions aside, libel is hurtful and morally wrong.

To defend a libel charge you must prove that what you wrote was true, and the best way to do that is with documentation. The second-best way is with witnesses.

If somebody grants you a private interview and makes a statement that shows him up as dishonest, bigoted, foolish, unfaithful to his wife, or anything else for which people may condemn him, you had better not quote him by name. You have no proof that he made the statement. (Even if you tape-record him, he can later claim you faked his voice.)

If he makes the same statement to you and a couple of other people, you are on safer ground — provided you are sure those other people will back you up. If they are the interviewee's employees, friends or family members, your safest course is to assume they won't back you up — and, once again, you had better not use the statement with the interviewee's name.

If he writes the statement in a magazine article, for example, or says it on a television talk show, then you are perfectly safe in using it. You have documentation.

Similarly, be very careful about leveling accusations of wrongdoing at people. If a man has been convicted in court of committing a crime, then you are safe. The conviction is a matter of public record, and you can write flatly, "So-and-so embezzled a million dollars from his company." If he is merely charged with the crime but not convicted, be sure to use the phrase "alleged," "charged with" or "police allege that . . ." And if no public charge has been made, don't use the individual's name at all. Don't ever repeat a charge made in private. Don't write, "Acording to Nancy Smith, a secretary in the highway commissioner's office, the commissioner regularly accepts bribes from construction companies . . ." You cannot escape responsibility for the libelous statement by putting the burden on Nancy Smith. She has committed slander, but you, the writer, have committed libel.

Your only defense against the highway commissioner's wrath in this case would be to obtain solid evidence that the alleged bribes actually took place. That, of course, would be a very tough reporting assignment. If you are writing the kind of book in which you must make statements about wrongdoing, hide the identity of individuals who haven't been convicted or publicly charged. Instead of "Nancy Smith" and "the highway commissioner," make it "a secretary" and "a high-placed public official." This technique, of course, will put extra pressure on you to preserve the ring of truth.

How long should I save my research file, manuscript carbon, rough draft and other material?

You can throw out your rough draft and carbon copies as soon as the book is published — unless, of course, they have some sentimental value for you.

As for your research file, keep it forever. There are a number of good reasons for doing this. In the first place, you will need documentation and witnesses' names in the unlikely event that somebody makes a formal complaint about something you have written or (still more unlikely) sues you and the publisher for libel. Such a complaint could arise years after the book is published.

In the second place, you will find yourself answering letters and phone calls from readers for years after the book is published. Readers will want to know all kinds of things: addresses of people you've mentioned in the book, opinions and advice on various aspects of your subject. This task of answering reader mail (your publisher will forward it to you) is somewhat irritating, but it is part of the nonfiction game. If a reader has paid $5.95 or more for your book and is interested enough to pursue the subject further, you have a certain moral obligation to give him the help he asks for.

But probably the best reason for saving research materials is that this subject of yours, in all likelihood, will continue to live as potential nonfiction material in the years ahead. You may decide to write a new, updated version of the book at some future time, or you may want to write a different book that peripherally touches the first book's subject matter or looks at it from a fresh new angle. (Indeed, your publisher may ask you to do so.) In addition, it is entirely possible that magazine and newspaper editors will ask you to write short pieces about certain aspects of your subject. Having written a book, you are automatically considered (though you humbly doubt it) an expert on this particular subject.

Saving bulky research files can become a nuisance, but your files are potentially valuable, perhaps much more valuable than you can now foresee. If you wouldn't throw out a $100 watch, don't throw out a file that could be worth a lot more.

It sounds exciting — and maybe profitable, too.

Exciting it is. Profitable? I make you no promises. But remember that every successful nonfiction book writer in the business today was once a beginner. Each, at some time in the past, had to write his first book without being able to see the future. Each had to sustain himself, for a while, largely on his own faith. He believed he was a good writer, though perhaps nobody else did at the time, and he set out to prove it.

The act of faith and the process of justifying the faith are both exhilarating. As for fame and fortune, who knows? The literary world gives nobody a written guarantee. No writer can ever see his own future except in his dreams. But the dreams themselves can be great fun.